# Into Slavery
# Racial Decisions in the
# Virginia Colony

Michael Les Benedict
    The Fruits of Victory: Alternatives in Restoring the
    Union, 1865-1877

Joseph Boskin
    Into Slavery: Racial Decisions in the Virginia
    Colony

David M. Chalmers
    Neither Socialism nor Monopoly: Theodore
    Roosevelt and the Decision to Regulate the Rail-
    roads

Roger Daniels
    The Decision to Relocate the Japanese Americans

Richard O. Davies
    The Age of Asphalt: The Automobile, the Free-
    way, and the Condition of Metropolitan America

Lloyd C. Gardner
    Wilson and Revolutions: 1913-1921

Warren F. Kimball
    Swords or Ploughshares? The Morgenthau Plan
    for Defeated Nazi Germany, 1943-1946

Ernest R. May
    The Truman Administration and China, 1945-1949

Jane H. and William H. Pease
    The Fugitive Slave Law and Anthony Burns: A
    Problem in Law Enforcement

J. R. Pole
    The Decision for American Independence

Robert A. Rutland
    Madison's Alternatives: The Jeffersonian Republi-
    cans and the Coming of War, 1805-1812

Darrett B. Rutman
    John Winthrop's Decision for America: 1629

Anne F. and Andrew M. Scott
    One Half the People: The Fight for Woman Suf-
    frage

Robert Sobel
    Herbert Hoover at the Onset of the Great Depres-
    sion, 1929-1930

Theodore Thayer
    Yorktown: Campaign of Strategic Options

Hans L. Trefousse
    Lincoln's Decision for Emancipation

Wilcomb E. Washburn
    The Assault on Indian Tribalism: The General
    Allotment Law (Dawes Act) of 1887

# Joseph Boskin

Boston University

## The America's Alternatives Series

Edited by Harold M. Hyman

# Into Slavery

## Racial Decisions in the Virginia Colony

J. B. Lippincott Company

Philadelphia/New York/San Jose/Toronto

ISBN 0-397-47347-8
Library of Congress Catalog Card Number
Printed in the United States of America

1 3 5 7 9 8 6 4 2

Library of Congress Cataloging in Publication Data

Boskin, Joseph.
   Into slavery.

   (America's alternatives series)
   Bibliography: p.
   1. Slavery in the United States—Virginia.
2. Virginia—Politics and government—Colonial
period, ca. 1600-1775. 3. Slavery in the United
States—Virginia—Sources. 4. Virginia—Politics
and government—Colonial period, ca. 1600-1775—
Sources. I. Title.
E445.V8B64     301.44'93'09755     75-31995
ISBN 0-397-47347-8

In the struggles of working-class life
they fought for every sprig in the street
and gave each to their sons . . .
my parents, Dina and Abraham Boskin

# Contents

Foreword ix
Acknowledgments xi

PART ONE    Into Slavery    1
Introduction    3

1    The Indian and the Servant    6
*The Stage    6        Early Expectations: Indian as Student
and Convert    7        Narrowing the Options: Indian as
Enemy and Outcast    10        White Servitude        14*

2    The Education    18
*Perpetuating Englishness    18        Bulwarks Against
Savagery    20        Education and the African    23*

3    The Name    26
*British Attitudes Towards Blackness    26        Denying
the African his Name    28        Renaming in the English
Image    32        The Impact of Namelessness    34*

4    The Decisions, The Laws    38
*Judicial Decisions: Towards a Legal Status as Slave    38
The Legal Problem of the Nonwhite Christian    40
Economic and Legislative Trends towards Slavery    42
Narrowing Options for Freedom    46*

EPILOGUE:    The Gestalt    51

PART TWO    Documents of the Decision    55

1    Savage    57

2    William Crashaw's Sermon, 1610    58

3    Civility    61

4    Of the Naturall Inhabitants of Virginia    63

5    A Brief Description of the People, May 21-June 21, 1607
     64

6    Instructions to George Yeardley, 1618    66

7    Report of the Treasurer on Funds for Henrico College,
     1619    67

8    John Smith's Thoughts on the Massacre    69

9    Laws of Virginia, 1623-1624    70

10   A Declaration of the State of the Colonie and Affairs in
     Virginia    72

11   Indian Education, Connecticut, 1654    74

12   "They are not Deficient in Natural Understanding"    75

13   Laws of Virginia, December, 1656    78

14   Laws of Virginia, September, 1632    80

15   Duke's Law of the State of New York, 1664    81

16   "Of Children and Their Education"    82

17   A Proposition for Encouraging the Christian Education
     of Indian, Negro, and Mulatto Children    87

18   Contract for Negroes, 1642    88

19   Narrative of Olaudah Equiano    89

20   Laws of Virginia, March, 1661-1662    90

21   Laws of Virginia, October, 1669    91

22   Laws of Virginia, October, 1670    92

23   Laws of Virginia, June, 1680    93

24   Laws of Virginia, November, 1682    94

25   Laws of Virginia, April, 1691    96

PART THREE    Bibliographic Essay    99

Index    113

# Foreword

"When you judge decisions, you have to judge them in the light of what there was available to do it," noted Secretary of State George C. Marshall to the Senate Committees on the Armed Services and Foreign Relations in May 1951.[1] In this spirit, each volume in the "America's Alternatives" series examines the past for insights which History—perhaps only History—is peculiarly fitted to offer. In each volume the author seeks to learn why decision makers in crucial public policy or, more rarely, private choice situations adopted a course and rejected others. Within this context of choices, the author may ask what influence then-existing expert opinion, administrative structures, and budgetary factors exerted in shaping decisions? What weights did constitutions or traditions have? What did men hope for or fear? On what information did they base their decisions? Once a decision was made, how was the decision-maker able to enforce it? What attitudes prevailed toward nationality, race, region, religion, or sex, and how did these attitudes modify results?

We freely ask such questions of the events of our time. This "America's Alternatives" volume transfers appropriate versions of such queries to the past.

In examining those elements that were a part of a crucial historical decision, the author has refrained from making judgments based upon attitudes, information, or values that were not current at the time the decision was made. Instead, as much as possible he or she has explored the past in terms of data and prejudices known to persons contemporary to the event.

1. U.S., Senate, Hearings Before the Committees on the Armed Services and the Foreign Relations of the United States, *The Military Situation in the Far East*, 82d Cong., 2d sess., part I, p. 382. Professor Ernest R. May's "Alternatives" volume directed me to this source and quotation.

Nevertheless, the following reconstruction of one of America's major alternative choices speaks implicitly and frequently, explicitly to present concerns.

In form, this volume consists of a narrative and analytical historical essay (Part One), within which the author has identified by use of headnotes (i.e., Alternative 1, etc.) the choices which he believes were actually before the decision makers with whom he is concerned.

Part Two of this volume contains, in whole or part, the most appropriate source documents that illustrate the Part One Alternatives. The Part Two Documents and Part One essay are keyed for convenient use (i.e., references in Part One will direct readers to appropriate Part Two documents). The volume's Part Three offers users further guidance in the form of a Bibliographic Essay.

Professor Boskin's *Into Slavery* carves a clear path through the heavily encrusted literature on the origins and characteristics of American Negro slavery. Now the beginnings of the black Americans' time on the cross are more clearly set down, so that tenacious and sometimes footnoted myths about these beginnings may, hopefully, be corrected. Until this correction occurs, our understanding will remain defective, and subject to exploitative misdirection, about the ways in which the land of the free became also the home of the slave. No question to which historians address themselves is more important than this. Its numerous impacts on race relationships since 1607 are central concerns of American society in 1976. The bicentennial commemoration is a particularly fitting time for a close re-examination of these essential matters, of the sort *Into Slavery* provides.

Harold M. Hyman
Rice University

# Acknowledgments ━━━━

I have been touched by many persons in the writing of this book. Sometimes their very presence, sometimes a word or a nudge, other times a helpful note or insightful suggestion, and on occasion a biting criticism, these unseen actions have made possible the completion of this work. I am particularly grateful to Murray Levin for his "symphonies" of humor and perspective; to Sidney Burrell for his open door of support; to Adelaide Gulliver for her generous scholarly assistance; to Richard Newman for a constant flow of information; to David Hall for his spontaneous offerings of bibliographical leads; to Gary Nash for his eager willingness to make available manuscript materials; to William Applegate for a cheerful demeanor towards a certain drudgery; to Harold Hyman and Lee Gudel for their gentle criticisms.

Further, without the feel of Claire for her quest into unique pathways; the bond of Joel Tarr; the poetic flow of Deena Metzger; the unspoken tie to Barbara Myerhoff; the curiosity of Arnold Shapiro; the intense search of Stan Wachs; the joyous support of Susan Eckstein; the prodding of Sam Bass Warner; the playful imageries of Renee and Roger Gould; the creative drives of Polia and William Pillin; the spriteful conversations of Rita and Max Lawrence; the long embrace of Cheri Pann and Robert Rosenstone; the entwining struggle of Barbara Filo; and the restless energy of Helen and Sheldon Benjamin: without them I could not have made it to this moment.

# Part One

# Into Slavery

# Introduction

# The Problem: Development of an Equation

"These two words, *Negro* and *Slave*, being by custom grown Homogeneous and Convertible . . . "

Morgan Godwyn, *The Negro's and Indian Advocate, Serving for their Admission into the CHURCH Or A Persuasive to the Instructing and Baptising of the Negros and Indians in Our Plantations* (London, 1680), p. 36.

"Generally speaking," Alexis de Tocqueville acutely observed in the early part of the nineteenth century as he analyzed race relations in the United States against the backdrop of History:

men must make great and unceasing efforts before permanent evils are created; but there is one calamity which penetrated furtively into the world, and which was at first scarcely distinguishable amid the ordinary abuses of power: it originated with an individual whose name history has not preserved; it was wafted like some accursed germ upon a portion of the soil; but afterwards nurtured itself, grew without effort, and spread naturally with the society to which it belonged. This calamity is slavery.[1]

So it was with the gradual establishment of slavery in the North American colonies in the seventeenth century. Though the English possessed ideas and images about dark-skinned people, enslavement as a policy was not an object of settlement. Nor was the destruction of such people an aim of the original colonists. Yet, within an incredibly short space of time, both policies became an integral part of custom, attitudes, stereotypes, and law. Of the two distinct cultural groups with whom the English interacted in the New World, the Indian was eventually destroyed, the African gradually enslaved.

The slave system emerged in the 1660s and '70s in Virginia and Maryland with the enactment of major laws which reflected the predominant attitudes towards Negroes. These laws provided for lifelong servitude for blacks as contrasted with whites and Indians; discounted baptism as a means for changing slave status to free status; decreed that a child would inherit its mother's social position; and, with strong sanctions, prohibited intermarriage.

3

Thereafter, a body of written and unwritten law arose to define precisely the status of enslaved blacks. The ultimate consequence of these actions was the designation of blacks as chattel property. Once defined basically as bondsmen, they had severely restricted rights and powers and could be bought, sold, and punished with virtual impunity (*Alternative 3: Lifelong Slavery; Alternative 4: Perpetual Slavery*).

In the northern colonies as well, slave legislation was enacted for the African. Although not as detailed as those laws of Virginia and Maryland, they nevertheless had the identical effect of a social and psychological equation which rested upon a racial foundation: white connoted freedom, black symbolized slavery. In societal terms, this meant that the servant was always white and the slave inevitably black. Morgan Godwyn, who argued in favor of admitting Negroes and Indians into the church in 1680, noted the power of this equation:

> These two words, *Negro* and *Slave*, being by custom grown Homogeneous and Convertible; even as *Negro* and *Christian, Englishman* and *Heathen*, are by the like corrupt custom and Partiality made *opposites;* thereby as it were implying that the one could not be *Christians*, nor the other *Infidels*. [2]

These actions were not accidental nor inevitable. The English were generally familiar with Spanish behavior in the Carribbean region and in South America but there was no concept of chattel slavery in England itself. In seventeenth-century England, as Oscar and Mary Handlin have noted in their treatment of the problem, the laws recognized gradations of servility, the lowest position being not one of slave but of relative "unfreedom" (*Alternative 2: Degrees of Unfreedom*). No person was outside the pale of society; that is, no English person. [3]

Furthermore, extensive interactions with other civilizations were usually not direct but were made in the course of maritime activities. In the initial contact with both the Indian and African, there was fluidity and openness. It could have been anticipated that when these groups encountered each other there would be social conflict. Yet, within the process of conflict, options did exist. Choices were to be made within circumstances that had to be analyzed and defined. Decisions did not become fixed until the options were narrowed, customs determined, and a recognition of the lack of choice was accepted.

If choices did exist for the English in their early contacts with the Indian and African, what transpired to create a situation of intense hostility which led to a system of enslavement? Shortly after their arrival on the eastern shores of the continent, the English became the predominant group, quickly expanding their base and power. Consequently, they were in a position to define and determine intergroup relationships. Why, then, did the English depart from their early recognition of Indian sovereignty? With respect to the African, despite the different basis upon which they related, why did the English not assimilate them into their society? In short, why didn't the English accommodate both the Indian and African within a social order which by custom and law would define and protect their status, rights and properties? (*Alternative 1: Total Assimilation*).

When the English settler imprinted the status of slave upon the African in one form or another and developed a program of destruction against the Indian, another and different dimension of the English character was developed. Their decisions represented the termination of a situation of options. At least the English *assumed* that they had no other choice but to commit themselves to certain policies in relation to the other races. Separation and segregation consequently became policies which were pronounced in custom and law but emanated from similar motivations. Daniel Bell explained this development as arising from the "moral sensibilities and temper" of a people. "To see history," Bell has argued,

> as changes in sensibilities and style, or more, how different classes of people mobilized their emotional energies and adopted different moral postures is relatively novel; yet the history of moral temper is, I feel, one of the most important ways of understanding social change, and particularly the irrational forces at work in men.[4]

Though the interchange between the English and Indian would reflect and affect the relationship which occcurred between the English and African, this work is primarily concerned with the latter. It specifically focuses on the development of an equation which permanently separated English from African, white from black, servant from slave, free from bond. Between the years 1619-1660, laws and practices were developed which laid the foundation for slavery and the status of a slave as chattel property.

Why didn't the English assimilate the African into their culture in the first four decades before the crushing legislation of the 1660s and 1670s *(Alternative 1)?* Why were not serious attempts made to educate the African to English perceptions of law, manners, customs, and habits? Why didn't the English incorporate black men and women into the fold and resolve the social conflict in terms of a degree of "unfreedom" rather than slavery *(Alternative 2)?* In short, why didn't the English permit the African to become dark Englishmen?

It would appear that consciously or unconsciously the question which presented itself before the English time and again in those early years of contact was: can this person become like Me? like Us? Slowly at first, but more quickly as contact increased, the response evolved from scrutiny to *no (Alternative 3: Lifetime Slavery),* then to *never (Alternative 4: Perpetual Slavery).* That *never* has been America's social tragedy for over three centuries.

## Notes

1. Alexis de Tocqueville, *Democracy in America* (1835; New York: Random House, Vintage Books, 1945), vol. 1, p. 371.

2. Morgan Godwyn, *The Negro's and Indian Advocate, Serving for their Admission into the CHURCH or A Persuasive to the Instructing and Baptising of the Negros and Indians in our Plantations* (London, 1680), p. 36.

3. Oscar and Mary Handlin, "The Origins of the Southern Labor System," *William and Mary Quarterly*, 3rd ser., vol. 7 (April, 1950), p. 203, n. 16.

4. Daniel Bell, *The End of Ideology* (New York: Free Press, 1961), p. 440, n. 169.

# 1

# The Indian and The Servant

> "The entire man is, so to speak, to be seen in the cradle of the child."
>
> "The growth of nations presents something analogous to this; they all bear some marks of their origin. The circumstances that accompanied their birth and contributed to their development affected the whole term of their being."
>
> Alexis de Tocqueville,
> *Democracy in America*, 1835

## The Stage

Separation and contact, hostility and cooperation, miscegenation and marriage, confronting and gaming, riots and counterrevolts: a history of continuous and seemingly repetitious opposites characterizes the nature of race behavior in American society. Like the colors of black and white, the interaction between the two major races in the United States has been marked by polarities. Living together/apart reflects the social order which has been an integral part of the culture from the earliest contact between the African and English. What was past remains consistently present; what was then affects us now.

Opposites also characterize the motivations of those who migrated to the eastern seaboard in the seventeenth century. For many years Europeans viewed the unexplored lands in the Western Hemisphere with enormous expectations and imagined dangers. Within the sparsely settled territory was the opportunity to escape from structure, restrictions and withholding ideas. Conversely, within the sparsely settled territory was the chance to replant traditional structures, institutions, and ideas. Freedom and fear, purpose and the gamble were feelings and motives which crisscrossed and contradicted each other.

Complex and diverse communities reflected the variety of personal commitments and backgrounds in the colonial period. Communities were not monolithic but relatively open and dynamic. The English "had moved farther along than any other Western power toward conceiving of colonies, not as exploitative bands of transient men, but as permanent, self-sustaining communities," wrote Lawrence Cremin in his authoritative work on

6

education in American society. It was also clear that the contact between the Indian, African, and English contributed to a greater heterogeneity. The amalgam of the three cultures, as Cremin further observed, enhanced the quality of diversity in the colonies. "Diversity, therefore, and with it the attendant phenomena of cultural competition, accommodation, and blending, was from the very beginning a fundamental fact of American life."[1]

Prejudgments, however, play no small role in the determination of group policies and relationships. The English clearly possessed certain conceptions about themselves and other cultures; and, inasmuch as they quickly became the predominant culture, it is not surprising that attempts were made to define Indians and Africans in relation to Englishmen and women, to their environment, and to their preconceptions about other cultures. Conflict between these diverse cultures arose with the translation of these definitions into social, economic, and religious interactions. Conflict, apparently, was inevitable. If "we recognize the fact," wrote Brewton Berry in *Race and Ethnic Relations*, "that conflict involves also those subtle, restrained forms of interaction wherein one seeks to reduce the status of one's opponent, and not to eliminate him entirely from the conflict, then perhaps it is true that conflict invariably occurs when unlike peoples meet."[2]

Not only did the three cultures meet on uneven grounds, but the environment was unstable as well. To establish and create a new community—twentieth-century sociologists have noted that it takes many years for a newly developed suburban community to stabilize itself—requires intense direction, determination, and ideology. A crucial factor in the determination of group relationships, particularly as it related to the more powerful English, was their limited experience. Unlike the Portuguese and Spanish, whose histories had intersected with the North Africans over many centuries, the English had remained relatively isolated from diverse, nonwhite societies. Sailors and traders had come into contact with dark-skinned peoples but the British population had limited experiences and secondhand information about them. One of the cultural consequences of this separation, along with other influences, was the development of an acute sense of national identity, a powerful ethnocentrism.

For a people who had led a singularly circumscribed existence relative to other races, the presence of two disparate groups must have been rather difficult. Given the hardships and challenges of the environment and the constant tension of dealing with new problems, the situation was hardly propitious for mutual sensitivity.

## Early Expectations: Indian as Student and Convert

Of the two ethnic cultures encountered in their first two decades of settlement, the English were more prepared to deal with the Indian than the black. Long before John Rolfe wrote in his diary, "About the last of August [1619] came in a dutch man of warre that sold us twenty negars," the English had made plans for establishing relationships with the North

American Indian. Intent upon developing hegemony, they hoped to create a situation within which there would exist a modicum of cultural and trade interchange, bringing economic rewards to themselves but also religious and educative blessings to the Indian.

Within the framework of English thought there existed a "dual vision" or "split image" of the basic nature and capability of the Indian. "On the one hand," explained Gary B. Nash in a comparative analysis treating the development of racism in colonial society, "the native was imagined to be a savage, hostile, beastlike creature who inhabited the animal kingdom rather than the kingdom of man" (see Document 1). Concomitantly, the Indian was also perceived as having a gentle nature, childlike and innocent, open and tractable, and within the reaches of civility and civilization.[3]

In an attempt to resolve the dichotomy of their perceptions and to bring the Indian closer to the English ways of worship and thinking, the English spelled out specific plans and desires. Settlers received instructions regarding their actions. The *Letters Patent of the Virginia Charter* of 1606, using language which was to be repeated twice within the next six years in other charters, took cognizance of the presence of the Indian and directed the colonists in their responsibilities:

> . . . WE greatly commending, and graciously accepting of, their desires for the furtherance of so noble a work, which may, by the providence of Almighty God, hereafter tend to the Glory of his divine Majesty, in propagating of Christian religion to such people, as yet live in darkness and miserable ignorance of the true knowledge and worship of God, and may in time bring the infidels and savages, living in those parts, to human civility, and to a settled and quiet government . . .[4]

The royal charter and instructions from the crown thus reflected the intense desires of the nation to sustain and to impart a particular way of life, one felt to be intimately related to economic and spiritual salvation for the settlers and their future children.

Sermons repeated the directives with strong emphasis, indicating a fear that in the process of separation a breakdown of purpose would occur. ". . . Remember thou art a Generall of English men," exhorted William Crashaw in 1610, on the occasion of the departure of Lord Delaware, "nay a Generall of Christian men; therefore principally looke to religion." Crashaw pointed the way: "You goe to commend it to the heathen, then practice it yourselves: make the name of Christ honourable, not hatefull unto them (see Document 2).

The English were directed not merely to exploit the environment and to create a new society, but also to carry the fruits of English civilization to those who lived in darkness, without the faith, without a settled and quiet government, and without the trappings of civilized beings *(Alternative 1:* see Document 3). The Indians were such creatures, their very existence an example of innocence and savagery. To elevate them to a higher plane was a dream nurtured by many officials and others with paternalistic motives, but it was a dream which was constantly jarred.

How was the Indian to receive knowledge of the faith and the ways of civilized beings? The instruments were the institutions of church and school. Education, though not the only means to be employed, was to be the primary path to familiarity and perhaps acculturation. An educated Indian would not only be able to partake of English culture but would also be able to return to the tribe as a missionary. Methods of bringing the gospel and culture to the Indian were discussed in advance of settlement. Here, too, there was a duality in English thinking. Richard Hakluyt, the extraordinary compiler of the English voyages and navigations, counselled the members of the Virginia Company in 1609 in their approach to the Indian:

> ... To handle them gently, while gentle courses may be found to serve, it will be without comparison the best: but if gentle polishing will not serve, the one shall not want hammerours and rough masons enow, I meane our old soldiers trained up in the Netherlands, to square and prepare them to our Preachers hands.[5]

Further, to prevent Indian priests, the "Iniocasockes," from obstructing efforts in this area, the council of the London Company at various times suggested that they be detained as prisoners if necessary, or if proven to be "willful and obstinate," three or four of them should be transported to England for their unhampered conversion to the faith.[6]

In the eyes of the English, there were other difficulties which complicated the process. "They are inconstant in everie thing," John Smith wrote of the natural inhabitants of Virginia, "but what feare constraineth them to keepe." Smith also advised of their opposite traits: "Craftie, timerous, quicke of apprehension and very ingenuous. Some are of disposition fearfull, some bold, most cautelous, all Savage" (see Document 4).

Specific projects for educating Indians, particularly children, were endorsed early in the seventeenth century by the crown, philanthropic persons, and members of the clergy. The training of children was to be the principal channel through which the English would accomplish their objectives. "Take their children and traine them up with gentlenesse," it was directed in 1612, "teach them our English tongue, and the principles of religion; ... In steed of Iron and steele you must have patience and humanitie to manage their crooked nature to your form of civilitie."[7] Other documents expressed the need of "trayning and bringing up of Infidells children to the true knowledge of God and understanding of righteousness."[8]

Optimism characterized early activities. Some of the colonists were impressed with the Indians' educative abilities. In a detailed account of their behavior written in 1607, a settler concluded that "they are a very witty and ingenious people, apt both to understand and speake our language ..." (see Document 5).

Institutional efforts took various forms. One was to select boys with certain levels of intelligence and "graces of nature," instruct them in religion and civility, prepare them for a college, and return them to their people as converts. Troubles developed, however, when Indians balked at parting with their sons. A second method was to bring entire families to live with the

English. They were to be given a house, land, and cattle. The numbers, however, were to be limited because of a fear of collective violence. This plan was carried out on a minimal scale but abandoned after the Indian attack on the colony in 1622, an uprising which gave credence to English anxieties. A more complex undertaking was a third approach, to construct a college for the Indian. Serious efforts towards this goal were not begun until 1617 when James I sent a communication to the archbishops to work towards "some Churches and Schooles for *ye* education of *ye* children to those Barbarians" (*Alternative 1:* see Document 6).[9]

For the next two years a collection was made for the purchase of ten thousand acres for a university and college at Henrico, Virginia for the conversion of Indian youths. Other contributions flowed into the endowment for the institution in the form of funds, books, and goods. While the company was preparing the ground for the building of the college—one hundred tenants were transported in 1619 to cultivate the land at Henrico, their rewards being one-half of the land—funds from individual sources were made available to educate Indian children in private homes. A financial donation left by an individual, for example, which provided for the instruction of Indian boys "in the grounds of Christian religion" at the college, was set aside for the care of three children every year. By 1621, plans were formulated and directors were actively involved in the establishment of the college for religious and civic ends. It was a missionary effort representative of individuals who possessed a sense of divine worth and power, who were convinced that the mind and spirit were linked, and who were certain that through children lay the salvation of the generations (see Document 7).

## Narrowing the Options: Indian as Enemy and Outcast

But the project never materialized. Relations between the Indians and English quickly deteriorated as members of each culture became disgruntled with the behavior of the other. As the colony around Jamestown and Williamsburg settled into permanency and acquisition of land became the primary objective, the dual vision of the Indian was no longer functional. The Englishman began to view his neighbor solely as hostile and savage. As Gary Nash has acutely observed, there occurred in those first years of settlement and contact, "a subconscious attempt to manipulate the world in order to make it conform to the English definition of it." The stereotype of the violence-prone savage "helped assuage a sense of guilt which inevitably arose when men whose culture was based on the concept of private property embarked on a program to dispossess another people of their land."[10]

Conflict intensified as attitudes hardened in other areas as well. Nancy Oestreich Lurie, in assessing the positive and negative responses of the English, has noted that in certain crucial areas, the Indian was denied respect: "The Indian won the grudging respect of the colonists for their advanced technology, but the Europeans were contemptuous of their seemingly hopeless commitment to superstition, while their ceremonalism appeared to the whites as a ridiculous presumption of dignity."[11]

To the Indian, however, the inexorable advance of the newcomers posed a threat to their game supply and to their land. Hostilities flared into sporadic outbursts of violence. While arrangements for Henrico College were seriously underway in England and Virginia, the Indians, goaded by anxiety, attacked the settlements in 1622 with a fierceness that convinced the Virginia colonists that civilized existence was beyond the "savages." One-third of the colony was wiped out, including members of the council and other prominent and experienced settlers.

Decisions and practices enacted after the attack signalled the end of cordial relationships and of the English hope for the spiritual redemption of the Indian. In their place were instituted policies of retaliation and expulsion. John Smith noted that the episode provided the rationale for a policy of destruction and subjugation for some people in the colony. Ironically, he was unconvinced because the Indians "have given us an hundred times as just occasions long agoe to subject them (see Document 8)."[12]

The ordinances came swiftly. In addition to the prohibition against public and private trading of corn, the assembly ordered,

That every dwelling house shall be pallizaded in for defence against the Indian.
That no man go or send abroad without a sufficient partie well armed.
That men go not to worke in the ground without their arms (and a centinell upon them).

Six acts followed in succession, each detailing another aspect of defense against future Indian attacks. A seventh provision, however, set in motion a strategy of counterattack which had begun the previous year:

That at the beginning of July next the inhabitants of every corporation shall fall upon their adjoyning salvages as we did the last yeare.

Disabled colonists, it was decreed, were "to be cured at the publique charge" while those who were lamed were "to be maintained by the country according to his person and quality." Six years later, this policy of constant warfare was enunciated in strong terms:

That the warr begun upon the Indians be effectually followed, and that noe peace be concluded with them (see Document 9).

Devastation of Indian fields and villages was countenanced; a scorched earth policy was devised. Options which had existed for the colonists—options which included trading, missionizing, and educating—were reduced to secondary considerations. Foremost was the reduction of the Indian as a military power, as an obstacle to expansion. "Because our hands which before were tied with gentlenesse and faire usage," wrote a Virginia spokesman after the violence of 1622,

are now set a liberty by the treacherous violence of the Savages, not untying the Knot, but cutting it: So that we, who hitherto have had possession of no more ground than their waste, and our purchase at a valuable consideration their owne contentment, gained; may now by right of Warre and law of Nations, invade the Country, and destroy them who sought to destroy us: whereby wee shall enjoy their cultivated places . . . and possessing the fruits of others labours. Now their cleared grounds in all their villages (which are situate in the fruitfullest places of the land) shall be inhabited by us, whereas heretofore the grubbing of woods was the greatest labour (see Document 10).

The duality of nature which had enabled the English to think in terms of exchanges was thus essentially ended and with it the possibility of a relationship on any term other than one of hostility or violence. If the Indian was beyond saving and uplifting, then alternatives were no longer feasible as within a realistic range of objectives.

Arrangements for formal schooling for the Indian after 1622 were continued but within a limited set of expectations. Efforts were meager and spotty, rarely going beyond missionary zealousness. Several techniques which had been used before the turning point were maintained. In the ensuing decades families were brought into the villages, Indian boys were educated at private expense, and exhortations for maintaining the vigil for future education were frequently heard in England and throughout the colonies. But on a large scale, the institutional thrust was basically ended in Virginia.

These attitudes were expressed in legislative enactments of the period. Laws relating to religious training significantly ignored the "savage." In 1632 the Virginia assembly passed specific legislation with regard to the religious instruction of "youth and ignorant persons." Nowhere was the Indian as such to be found in the statute which included children, servants, and apprentices. Ten years later the assembly passed similar legislation; again, the Indian was not mentioned. Then, in 1644, the Indians mounted another large attack and two years later the assembly did address itself to the issue of religious instruction for them. But the purpose was to reaffirm the previous laws by succinctly stating the *voluntary* nature of the process:

> And it is further enacted & consented, That such Indian children as shall or will freely and voluntarily come in and live with the English, may remain without breach of the articles of peace, provided they be not above twelve years old.[13]

Later legislation in the mid-1650s was more rhetorically direct in the area of education. Enactments dealing with servants in 1654 provided that

> all Indian children by leave of their parents shall be taken as servants for such a terme as shall be agreed on by the said parent and master as aforesaid; Provided that due respect and care be had that they the said Indian servants be educated and brought up in the Christian religion and the covenants . . .

Again, the proviso was based on voluntary actions. In another instance, because of the practice of kidnapping Indians "to the greate scandall of Christianitie," the assembly provided for the maintenance and education of Indian hostages, with an allowance of tobacco for each Indian when necessary.[14]

That Indian children were receiving various types of instruction, however, can be seen in the wording of a 1657 ordinance which dealt with their transference from one party to another. Indian children who were warded by their parents "either for education or instruction in Christian religion, or for learning the English tongue" could not be assigned to another person regardless of cause or length of service. The assembly was impressed with the initial reason for having Indian children so placed and decreed that "such Indian childe shall be free and at his owne disposall at the age of twenty five yeares." No such provision was ever made for African servants or slaves.

The voluntary format of education was continued throughout the latter half of the seventeenth century with uneven results. Even when some Indian tribes sought conversion, there was considerable suspicion of their lurking intention. The king of Pamunkey and many of his warriors, seeking Christianity and proper English names, were viewed by Lord Thomas Culpeper as "so trecherous that there is no trust in them." The lack of effort, save for continued bewailing from the concerned, was summed up by Governor Edmund Andros in 1697. Asked by the Board of Trade what steps were being taken for the conversion of Indians to the faith, he replied, "None ever heard of."[15]

Not until the early part of the eighteenth century was this noninstitutional pattern altered and by then it was too late. William and Mary College was the site for conversion and education. A number of Indian youths were so educated; however, the problem of their being sold as slaves prevented fathers from allowing their sons further to attend. A score of Indian boys captured in battles with hostile tribes were purchased by the colony and sent to the college or to another shortlived school. Assessment of the success of their education by contemporaries reflected ambivalence at best, and pessimism generally. The colonial attitude was summed up years earlier when a report from the London Company sternly noted: "The way of conquering them is much more easy than of civilizing them by fair means,

> for they are a rude, barbarous, and naked people, scattered in small companies, which are helps to victory, but hindrances to civility: Besides that, a conquest may be of many and at once: but civility is in particular, and, slow, the effects of long time, and great industry (see Document 10).

Efforts to educate the Indian were more pronounced in the northern colonies but the results did not bring about harmonious intercultural relationships. In New Amsterdam in 1636 the Dutch made specific mention of the need to establish schools for Indian children. The situation in Connecticut, however, was generally representative of Indian education in the region. A plan adopted in 1654 for "gospelizing" neighboring Indian tribes was constantly thwarted by warfare between the two groups (see Document 11).

The major accomplishments were in New England, where despite the Puritans' ambivalence concerning the ability of the Indian to be educated and religiously salvaged, an organized thrust was developed in the common schools and at Harvard College. In the mid-seventeenth century, English and Indian children attended common schools in Massachusetts; and at Harvard, a small group of Indian youths received an education. The numbers in all instances were never substantial and as Lawrence Cremin has pointedly noted in his significant work on the subject, the efforts at Harvard were "abysmal" mainly because of the "unspoken assumption that the Indians should aspire to the same social and cultural ends as the whites."[16]

Disillusionment with the Indian as a major convert to Christianity, to orderly government, and to civility and nonviolence was widespread throughout the colonies. The dream to educate the "infidels" resulted in frustration and anger. In the eighteenth century, the Society for the Propagation of the Gospel in Foreign Parts would seize the mantle of conversion. But by that time the Indian was regarded not merely as being beyond reason and order but also as an obstacle to westward expansion. As long as they existed the Indian would remain a constant reminder of what the English had avoided becoming—an example of a people trapped by the rudeness of the past and primitivism.

Frustrated in their pilgrimages to bring the riches of civilization to the Indians, the English essentially excluded them *(Alternative 2)*. There was no felt alternative to the Indians' status save as outcast. By the mid-eighteenth century, a sense of exasperation pervaded the colony regarding the "civilizing" of the Indian. Benjamin Franklin in 1753 summed up the attitude in half-mocking, ethnocentric terms:

> The proneness of human Nature to a life of ease, of freedom from care and labour appears strongly in the little success that has hitherto attended every attempt to civilize our American Indians, in their present way of living, about all their Wants are supplied by the spontaneous Productions of Nature, with the addition of very little labour, if hunting and fishing may indeed by called labour when Game is so plenty, they visit us frequently, and see the advantages that Arts, Sciences, and compact Society procure us, they are not deficient in natural understanding and yet they have never shown any Inclination to change their manner of life for ours, or to learning of our Arts; When an Indian Child has been brought up among us, taught our language and habituated to our Customs, yet if he goes to see his relations and make one Indian Ramble with them there is no persuading him ever to return . . . (see Document 12).

## White Servitude

The history of their relationship with the Indian was but one dimension of English attitudes which would impact upon the African. One of the demands of colonial economy was the requirement of large sources of labor. To meet the complexities of an expanding society, a system of white servitude was devised. 'Indentured servants'—labelled after the name of the contract which affixed transportation costs from England and a length of service—constituted more than half of all the persons who arrived in the colonies south of New England. Throughout the seventeenth century, this system was the sole means by which persons without resources could travel to the North American continent or by which white labor could be provided to the planters, farmers, speculators, and proprietors. Indeed, the tobacco economy of Virginia and Maryland was virtually dependent upon the labor of indentured servants.

Supplied mainly from the powerless classes in England—paupers, debtors, convicts, vagrants, political prisoners, hopefuls, apprenticed children, unemployed; in short, the alienated, disregarded, undesirable—they became the mainstay of the colonial labor force.[17]

The early experiences between the indentured servant and his or her owner had a profound effect upon other powerless groups in colonial society. It was "under the auspices of the Virginia Company that the customs and habits of indentured servants were established essentially in the forms which became so familiar to later colonial history."[18] Powerless indeed they were. Despite laws which afforded certain protection, bonded servants were often regarded as private property. The profit to be derived from the labor of the servants was immediately recognized. Wrote John Pory from Virginia in 1619, "Our principall wealth . . . consisteth in servants" and related how one planter with only six servants had profited a thousand pounds by a single crop of tobacco.[19] Ironically, 1619, the year that brought the first recorded large shipment of Africans to the colony, was the same year in which the guidelines of indentured servitude were fully developed. Throughout most of the century white servants remained the laborers upon which the tobacco economy rested, indicating the resistance of planters to substituting Africans as replacements.

From the very beginning, the thrust was towards status and power. Economic standing and wealth was to be accomplished through the accumulation of property, the development of which was to be achieved largely through labor. The servant was thus crucial to the enterprise of the individual and of the entire colony. To manipulate the labor source, to control it, became an important object. Of all the persons in Virginia in the early years, the servant was the most vulnerable, his condition worse in the colony than in England. Not only were the servants' terms longer than had been the case in England, but they were economically trapped. Their pay, for example, had been advanced in transportation costs. Exercising virtually no control over their own lives, servants were physically abused, sold to others without their consent, and constantly degraded.

Although white indentured servants received some support to ameliorate and improve their conditions by mid-century, they essentially remained unprotected in the colonies, their rights severely circumscribed. "The servant had rights, but while he was in servitude these rarely conflicted with the conception of him as property."[20] Masters had the power to regulate conduct, oversee performance of duties, direct freedom of action, conduct sales, and prescribe general behavior. Punishments for breaking laws, regulations, and whatever was regarded by individual masters as flouting their rules, were commonplace, the severity depending upon time, circumstance, and person. Heaviest punishment was given to those who tried to flee the system. To prevent loss resulting from runaways and to prevent retaliations, especially revolts, strict laws and reprisals were devised. "Virginia had been forced from its earliest years to take stringent steps against mutinous plots, and severe punishments for such behavior were recorded."[21] It is significant that most of these servant actions occurred in the seventeenth century, when their numbers were larger.

Though not property *per se*, the treatment servants received created an imbalance in the community, a distortion of energy and power in the propertied classes. For the practices and attitudes developed within the community towards fellow countrypersons could not augur well for other, more defenseless individuals. It is possible to observe in those boom years of the first decades, wrote Edmund Morgan, "Virginians beginning to move toward a system of labor that treated men as things."[22]

Given the attitude and behavior of those in power towards the indentured workers in the first half of the century, it is not surprising that similar expressions were directed towards the African. Being a heathen, black, and without the "indenture" or contract which gave meaning to a name, term of service, and other factors of identity, the African was in an even more powerless position. The foundation of ideas and concepts of servitude which were expressed in law and practices was not difficult to transfer to others who became part of the colony. Overall, it is clear that the impact of the white, indentured system was negative in relation to the status of nonwhites. "The tendency was to harden the master's feeling towards servitude and to prepare him for a more ready adoption of slavery, and the introduction of undesirable classes into a society already lax in habit was not likely to improve the moral tone or the social welfare of the colony."[23]

By virtue of introducing greater familiarities and contrasts, the African was placed in a more complex and precarious situation. Being in an indeterminate position, blacks were certain to be subjected to a greater scrutiny than either the Indian or white servant—for they were the true outsiders in the colony.

## Notes

1. Lawrence A. Cremin, *American Education: The Colonial Experience, 1607-1783* (New York: Harper & Row, 1970), p. 22.
2. Brewton Berry, *Race and Ethnic Relations* (New York: Houghton Mifflin, 1958), p. 122.
3. Gary B. Nash, "Red, White and Black: The Origins of Racism in Colonial America," in *The Great Fear: Race in the Mind of America* (New York: Holt, Rinehart & Winston, 1970), pp. 2-3.
4. William W. Hening, ed., *Statutes at Large: Being a Collection of all the Laws of Virginia from the First Session of the Legislature in the Year 1619* (1823; reprint ed., Charlottesville: University Press of Virginia, 1969), vol. 1, p. 58.
5. Sadie Bell, *The Church, the State, and Education in Virginia* (New York: Arno Press, 1969), p. 7.
6. W. Stitt Robison, Jr., "Indian Education and Missions in Colonial Virginia," *Journal of Southern History*, vol. 18, no. 2, pp. 153-54.
7. Bell, *The Church, the State, and Education*, p. 15.
8. S.M. Kingsbury, ed., *Records of the Virginia Company of London* (Washington, D.C.: Library of Congress, 1906), vol. 1, p. 220.
9. Bell, *The Church, the State, and Education*, p. 16.
10. Nash, "Red, White and Black," pp. 3-4.
11. Nancy Oestreich Lurie, "Indian Cultural Adjustment to European Civilization," in *Seventeenth Century America*, ed. James Morton Smith (Chapel Hill, N.C.: University of North Carolina Press, 1959), pp. 44-45.

12. Lyon Gardiner Tyler, ed., *Narratives of Early Virginia* (New York: Barnes & Noble, 1907), p. 99.

13. Hening, ed., *Statutes at Large*, vol. 1, pp. 180-181, 326.

14. Ibid., pp. 410, 480-81.

15. Robinson, "Indian Education," p. 161.

16. Cremin, *American Education*, pp. 194, 222.

17. Abbott E. Smith, *Colonists in Bondage* (Chapel Hill, N.C.: University of North Carolina Press, 1947), pp. 3, 20; James C. Ballagh, *White Servitude in the Colony of Virginia* (Burt Franklin, 1895), pp. 34-35.

18. Smith, *Colonists in Bondage*, p. 8.

19. Tyler, *Narratives of Early Virginia*, pp. 284-85.

20. Ibid., pp. 278-79.

21. Richard Hofstadter, *America at 1750* (New York: Alfred A. Knopf, 1971), p. 56.

22. Edmund S. Morgan, "The First American Boom: Virginia 1618-1630," *William and Mary Quarterly*, 3rd ser., vol. 28 (April, 1971), p. 198.

23. Ballagh, *White Servitude*, p. 90.

# 2

# The Education

> "So through remissness or ignorance on the part of parent and teacher, the minds of children may never be awakened to a consciousness of having, within themselves, blessed treasures of innate and noble faculties, far richer than any outward possessions can be; they may never be supplied with any foretaste of the enduring satisfactions of knowledge; and hence, they may attend school . . ."
>
> Horace Mann, First Annual Report,
> *On the Education of Free Men*, 1837

## Perpetuating Englishness

If the Indian could not be extricated from the ways of barbarism, what hope was there for the African? They were brought to the colonial shores stripped of name, family, community, and tribal identity, and virtually unable to communicate their past, worth, and status. To the English, they were the unknown quantity, related only to a heathen background. The problem posed by the tribal Indian was one of sharing contiguous lands and hunting areas while retaining separate identities. The problem posed by the presence of the tribal African was more demanding and complex; it was one involved with all the intricacies and subtleties attending relationships. Unlike the Indian who would live apart from the English, the African had to be accommodated to or assimilated into a culture which possessed a highly developed sense of ethnocentrism and images about others *(Alternative 1)*. It was therefore an educative process on the part of both the English and the African.

Moreover, this accommodation had to take place within a relatively unstable, disorderly environment. The overriding, complementary objectives of the first two generations in the colonies—the generations which would ultimately decide the positions of the Indian and African—were survival and the perpetuation of English culture. Not only was the harshness of the environment with its attendant dangers to be overcome, but individual relationships within the taut and confining communities had to be ameliorated and harmonized. The accommodative difficulties within the familial group were extensive. "In tight quarters of the seventeenth century," observed Oscar Handlin, "large families had to learn to live with one another, and also with the Negroes and other strange servants. Emotional strains were inevitable and weak community discipline sometimes led to violence, desertion, or criminality."[1]

The tautness of community life was reflected in the large number of cases brought before the colonial courts. All levels of society—landowners, servants, apprentices, churchmen, artisans, farmers, and others—turned to the courts in an attempt to define their positions, to make claims against others, and to determine the limits of personal and group action. The tradition of law was crucial to the colonists' survival in a situation of re-creation of community life and struggle for community control and direction.

But the law was not the only tradition the colonists relied on to establish stability and open avenues for redress and frustrations. Education was viewed as a primary means by which order could be created, the culture transmitted, and the heathens transformed in the English image. The courts would determine questions of right and power but education would determine questions of identity, morality, and inner worth.

Of all the western powers, the English alone utilized education as a unifying force in the development of colonial settlement and expansion. Education was a force which would hold society together and enable the younger generation to move in the direction expounded by the elders. As a force complimentary to both religious and economic motivations, education cannot be underestimated. Indeed, as Lawrence Cremin has pointedly noted, British superiority in the colonization process rested heavily upon their concept and institutionalization of education. Although English predominance was also the result of advanced technology, "the decisive influence of their culture was more than a matter of numbers or technology; it was in large measure a matter of education." Despite the fact that other western nations had transported families, established churches and missions, and set up schools, "none of these managed to develop education as extensively as the English."[2]

Soon after they arrived, the colonists quickly moved to maintain the essence of their culture. In New England, the town and church combined to aid the family in its efforts to retain the past, deal with the problems presented by the unique present, and prepare the children for the future. Efforts in the South were no less intense. Energies were mobilized to create an educative environment. Local and parish schools were established, servant-teachers were imported, and parents carefully provided for their children's education in their wills.

Concern for the education of youths was especially reflected in wills and court actions. Parents set aside large sums of money for education and religious instruction of their children, while courts administered supervision over orphans. A special session of the county court was held in each section at least once annually for the purpose of attending to matters pertaining to the welfare of children and in particular to the execution of orders relating to education. Those children without property were required to serve an apprenticeship and, by a clause inserted into the indenture, to receive instruction in reading, writing, and arithmetic from their masters. Children with property were required to obtain as full an education as possible.

The assembly in 1656 called for the instruction of orphans within the provisions of their estates but "if the estate be so meane and inconsiderable that it will not reach to a free education then that orphan be bound to some manuall trade till one and twenty years of age . . ." Friends or relations were permitted to keep the orphans; however, the principal of the estate was to remain unimpaired, no matter the size, and eventually returned to the person. The courts were directed to "enquire whether orphans be kept and maintained and educated" and to remove the guardians if these actions were not carried out (see Document 13).

An early example of a will which dealt with the subject was that of John Waltham, who died about 1640. Waltham directed that as soon as his son reached the sixth year, "instructions of good learning" should commence. He requested of his executors the names of some "good and godlye school-master" who would perform the important task. Other parents bequeathed property to ensure their children's education, or stipulated that the older children should direct the education of the younger ones.

Because of the newness of the circumstances and the contact with "savages," families were extraordinarily anxious to protect themselves and their children through formal and informal education. Bernard Bailyn has indicated that "the extravagance and often the impracticality of such efforts in Virginia, suggest a veritable frenzy of parental concern lest they and their children succumb to the savage environment." Direction arose from the tenuousness of the situation. "All their fearfullness for the consequences of transplantation, their awareness of the strangeness of the present and the perils of the future, seems to have become concentrated in the issue of education."[3]

Other related factors heightened the felt need. At the moment when the colonists sought for meaning in a system of education, they found themselves far from churches, schools, and colleges. Physical factors—the scattered farms and plantations separated by rivers and inlets—made the development of a structured system of education extremely difficult, creating a situation which compounded anxieties. A pamphlet of the period characterized these concerns: "Their almost general want of scholars for the education of their children is another consequence of their scattered planting of most sad consideration, most of all bewailed of parents there."[4] Morgan Godwyn, writing in 1680, also commented about the geography of schools and the relationship between the educational institution and civility: "And without a provision for Schools (of which the scattering way of living in these *Colonies* is scarce capable) together with a stricter Care taken to suppress Debauchery . . . may at least end in like Barbarity . . ."[5]

## Bulwarks Against Savagery

Legislation in Virginia and Massachusetts in the early 1630s and 1640s was designed to create an educational structure. In both colonies, the laws concentrated on the family unit as the unifying agency (see Document 14).

The Massachusetts law of 1642, one of the earliest statutes dealing with education, called attention to the "neglect of many parents and masters in training up their children in learning and labor" and directed those responsible to the duty of educating their children to the principles of religion and laws of society.[6] A Virginia law of 1646 instructed county officials to provide for children whose parents "by reason of their poverty are disabled to maintaine and educate them," and in New York in the mid-1660s, the Duke's Law contained similar admonitions (see Document 15).[7] Connecticut laws established similar guidelines, calling on parents and others to teach servants and children to read English, learn the capital laws, attain training in husbandry or some useful skill, and receive the catechism weekly. In most instances, parents and ministers were constantly counselled to send their children and servants for weekly religious instruction. Punishments of heavy fines enforced the legislation.

Informational education directives antedated the statutes. The colonial households in the early decades were forced to assume roles previously reserved to more established institutions. But apparently fear existed that the household might not be performing its now expanded task; hence legislative action to ensure its compliance in the rapidly changing circumstances.

Education as a vehicle of assimilation and acculturation mirrors the estimation of the worth of those to be educated. Moreover, those who view education as a critical standard of measurement and change are intimately concerned with the future. Education is thus the fusing of all history: the past which presents examples, the present which offers challenges, and the future which holds the hope of marked improvement.

English attitudes presumed that all persons, if they were to avoid the ways of savagery, must be educated. John Brinkley, noted schoolmaster in the reign of James I, presented to the Virginia Company his manuscript, "Consolations for Our Grammar Schools," in which he expressed the following attitude towards education: "God having ordained schooles of learning to be a principall meanes to reduce a barbarious people to ciulities." This approach was clearly directed towards the Indian, as well as others the British might encounter, but also related to children.

The connection between religious instruction and education, interwoven in English ideas, was clearly recognized in law. A Virginia statute of 1632 directed the minister to allow a half-hour or more before the evening prayer to "examine, catechise, and instruct the youth and ignorant persons to his parrish, in the ten commandments the articles of the belief and in the Lord's prayer." Fathers, mothers, masters, and mistresses were held responsible to "cause theire children, servants or apprentizes" who have not learned the catechism to come to the church at the "tyme appoynted, obedientlie to heare, and to be ordered by the mynister untill they have learned the same (see Document 14)." Punishment for all found to be in neglect of their duties was censure by the courts.[8] Similar pronouncements were found in many of the colonies. A typical example is the instruction and tone of a New Amsterdam law:

Whereas it is highly necessary and of great consequence that the youth from their childhood are well instructed in reading, writing, and arithmetic, and principally in the principles and fundamentals of the Christian religion . . . (see Document 15).

Concern about the failure of children to receive the necessary directive attention in religious and secular training and fear that they might devolve into barbarous savages led the British into an overprotective stance. The Indian example of heathenism and primitivism constantly served to prod the colonist into maintaining a vigil over education, while at the same time expressing the desire to save the Indian. But if the Indian could not be transformed or their ways ameliorated, at least English children could be saved and elevated.

Necessary parts of this system were proper guidance and authority figures. Within the close confines of community life, parents, tutors, ministers, and other surrogates set up formal and informal training for children. Their presence and example was regarded as crucial for the establishment of a proper Christian life and the prevention of savagery. The task, however, was perceived as an extremely difficult one. Children were apt to resist the process with considerable tenacity. John Robinson, in his 1625 work, "Of Children and their Education," argued that "surely there is in all children, though not alike, a stubbornness, and stoutness of mind arising from natural pride, which must, in the first place, be broken and beaten down; that so the foundation of their education being laid down in humility and tractableness, other virtues may, in their time, be built thereon." Robinson was insistent upon the elimination of these inherently wicked characteristics in order to prepare the child for learning. "This fruit of natural corruption and root of actual rebellion both against God and man must be destroyed, and no manner of way nourished, except we will plant a nursery of contempt of all good persons and things, and of obstinacy therein" (see Document 16).

Some three hundred years after these formulations regarding parental responsibility towards children's educational salvation were written, another Englishman expressed similar ideas. A modern perspective on British sentiments on the stubbornness and tenuous state of the child's mind can be found in William Golding's popular novel of the mid-1950s, *Lord of the Flies.* In Golding's setting, a group of British boys are isolated on a small island following a thermonuclear blast; there is no indication as to how they came to be there. They are all teenagers, males, and without elders. Bereft of adults, they soon separate into two antagonistic groups: one led by a boy who expresses goodness, rationality, a democratic order, and consensus; the other headed by a realist who asserts man's bestial nature. Although the majority of the boys are followers of the democratic leader, gradually they split off and join in the exultation of primitivism, symbolized by the ritual killing of a pig. Eventually the bulk of the boys become savagelike and begin the systematic destruction of the democratic followers, ultimately seeking out the leader himself. As the children-savages are hunting down the upholder of democracy, the last link with a civilized past, he, and presumably his destroyers, are "saved" by the reintroduction of the authority figure. The

British navy suddenly appears on the scene. An officer comes ashore, his first question to the democratic survivor indicating the hierarchy of social order: "Are there any adults—any grownups with you?"[9]

Three centuries earlier, colonists acted swiftly to prevent such a situation from occurring. Utilizing the family as the basic unit for the dissemination of knowledge and religion, buttressed by the church, school, and tutors, society geared itself to create stability, harmony, and a communal homogeneity. Although these efforts differed between the southern and northern settlements—geographic factors made for isolated communities in the former, for greater communication between institutions in the latter—energies invested in this direction were prodigious. In both instances, settlers had to contend with the Indian and African.

## Education and the African

If the intimate connections between Christianity, civility, and rationality, training and labor were achieved through the process of education, was the African included in the efforts? The English had anticipated the Indian and had mobilized finances, directives, and institutions to "civilize" and Christianize them. They had labored in the vineyards of education to transform the Indian, but the plantings had yielded meager fruit. Would these failures affect the African's situation? Would the African, whose presence was unanticipated, be among those to receive educational instruction—namely, youths, servants, apprentices, and Indians *(Alternative 1)?* Here was one of the first of various tests of options the colonists would face regarding black men and women.

From the evidence that exists, it would appear that from the earliest days of contact, the African was never made an integral part of the formal education arrangements. Although a small number of blacks were exposed to religious and secular training within the confines of the plantation and family life—the numbers are obscured—legislative provisions for their education do not appear before 1699, decades after the legalization of black slavery. Indeed, the words "Negro" and "slave" are conspicuously missing from the education statutes of the century. The omission is important, as these terms are to be found in the tax, defense, sex, religious, and census tracts of the period. Further perspective is added when one considers that the education of the Indian was specifically encouraged and provided for in legislative articles in many instances throughout the century, despite the enmity between the two peoples. But why was there little thought given to enacting such provisions for the African? A perusal of the statutes in such diverse colonies as Virginia, New York, Massachusetts, and others which deal with apprenticeship training reveals no mention of their bond or free Negroes and/or slaves. In almost all the settlments apprenticeship provisions appear with regularity as colonial attempts to provide for the learning and development of orphans, poor, and servants. The Virginia legislature did not provide for the compulsory education of mulatto children until 1765, at which time they were grouped with the orphaned, poor, and illegitimate children.[10] There were, however, educational clauses dealing with such training for the indentured children long before the passage of the law of 1765, but the frequency and extent of these practices is difficult to ascertain.

That some were concerned with the education of the black man can be seen by the actions of Reverend James Blair, who was responsible for the encouragement of educating Indian boys at William and Mary College. In "A Proposition for Encouraging the Christian Education of Indian, Negro, and Mulatto Children" in 1699, one of the few written exhortations involving black children, Blair called upon masters and mistresses "to endeavor the good instruction and education of their heathen slaves in the Christian faith . . .for the facilitating thereof among the young slaves that are born among us; that is, humbly proposed that every Indian, negro, or mulatto child that shall be baptized and afterward brought to church and publicly catechized by the minister in the church . . . (see Document 17). Though frequently discussed, Blair's proposition was apparently never enacted, and in any case, it appeared too late to have affected the slave status of the African. Scarcely a dozen years after the proposal, Bishop William Fleetwood of the Society for the Propagation of the Gospel in Foreign Parts, who had argued for the equal potentialities of the races, critically noted the disinterestedness of the colonists in this area:

> This unconcernedness of the Public it is, most probably, that encourages a great many private people at home amongst our selves to keep these *Africans,* or *Indians* in their native Ignorance and Blindness, and to continue the Infidels in the midst of a *Christian* Kingdom.[11]

Individual efforts to rectify the situation occurred throughout the seventeenth century, but they were uneven and unstructured. George Fox and George Keith counselled for the religious instruction of slaves, by which they meant the black workers. In a document extolling the benefits of the colony printed in 1649, "A Perfect Description of Virginia," there is an account from one individual who detailed the procedures by which slaves were to be taught artisan skills as well as the performance of simple manufacturing techniques. Prior to mid-century, some persons provided for the education and religious instruction of their black servants in their wills. Others, such as one Richard Vaughan, freed their black servants in 1654; "some of them he taught to read and make their own clothes." In addition to the stipulation that they be brought up in the fear of God, Vaughan left them property. But these actions were infrequent and dependent upon the whims of individual owners.[12] In short, as Cremin summarized, "as far as the blacks are concerned, it appears that only a handful attended school along with the whites, and there is no evidence at all of the establishment of any all-black schools."[13]

Thus, the British did not seriously entertain the idea of formally educating the African in the period which defined his place and position. Education as a technique of assimilating the African was apparently never considered and certainly not acted upon in any concerted manner. Such a crucial omission clearly pointed up the difficulty facing the African in his early interaction with the English. It may well be assumed that the African was regarded as uneducable.

The fact of educational exclusion resulted in a self-fulfilling process whereby the ignorance of blacks was interpreted as inferiority. Why, then, should energy and expenditure of funds be used to educate such people? Conversely, by placing fault on alleged imperfections, it was possible to keep blacks in a state of ignorance. In 1680 Morgan Godwyn recognized the circular reasoning of his day. ". . . the cause of Their Ignorance," he wrote of the Negro, "to be the want of Converse and Education . . ." One of the serious consequences of this exclusionist policy could be seen in the use of the English language by the Negro: " 'Tis true," Morgan noted, "the *Negro's* ignorance of our Language was for some times a real *Impediment* thereto . . ." Did the colonist use the "ignorance" of his language as a measurement of the African's abilities and reach negative conclusions?

Godwyn argued that such ignorance was no longer the case, for Negroes "had arrived to an ability of Understanding, and discoursing in *English* equal with most of our *own* People; which *many thousands* of them have long since have . . ." But by that time, the laws and custom of enslavement had been set. Blacks were not to be provided with the acutrements of education. Whatever they learned was haphazard, uneven, and sporadic. The equation of slave and ignorance, so vital to the perpetuation of the slave system, was firmly and early established.[14]

## Notes

1. Oscar Handlin, "The Significance of the Seventeenth Century," in *Seventeenth Century America,* ed. James Morton Smith (Chapel Hill, N.C.: University of North Carolina Press, 1959), p. 8.

2. Lawrence A. Cremin, *American Education: The Colonial Experience, 1607-1783* (New York: Harper & Row, 1970), pp. 22-24.

3. Bernard Bailyn, *Education in the Forming of American Society* (Chapel Hill, N.C.: University of North Carolina Press, 1960), pp. 28-29.

4. Philip A. Bruce, *Institutional History* (New York: G.P. Putnam's Sons, 1910), vol. 1, p. 294.

5. Morgan Godwyn, *The Negro's and Indian Advocate . . .* (London, 1680), p. 36.

6. Elsie Clews, *Educational Legislation and Administration of the Colonial Government* (New York: Macmillan Co., 1899), pp. 58-59.

7. Ibid., p. 223; William W. Hening, ed., *Statutes at Large . . .* (1823; reprint ed., Charlottesville: University Press of Virginia, 1969), vol. 1, p. 337.

8. Hening, *Statutes at Large,* p. 157.

9. William Golding, *Lord of the Flies* (New York: G.P. Putnam's Sons, Capricorn Books, 1959), p. 185.

10. Marcus W. Jernegan, *Laboring and Dependent Classes in Colonial America, 1607-1783* (Chicago, 1931), p. 169.

11. Frank J. Klingsberg, *Anglican Humanitarianism in Colonial New York* (Austin, Tx.: Church Historical Society, 1940), p. 209.

12. John H. Russell, *The Free Negro in Virginia, 1619-1865* (Baltimore: Johns Hopkins Press, 1913), pp. 137-38; Helen T. Catterall, *Judicial Cases Concerning American Slavery and the Negro* (New York: Octagon Books, 1968), p. 58; Jernegan, *Laboring and Dependent Classes,* pp. 10-11.

13. Cremin, *American Education,* pp. 194-95.

14. Godwyn, *The Negro's and Indian Advocate . . . ,* pp. 2, 36.

# 3

## The Name

"As his name is, so is he."

I Sam., 25:25

### British Attitudes Towards Blackness

The failure to incorporate the African into educational institutions indicates the English refusal to commit themselves to this crucial process. To what extent did this inaction reflect early English attitudes and practices in other areas? Is it possible to detect in the early behavior of the English the reasons which would lead to the exclusion of the African and their enslavement, and which would limit their options in dealing with the African? Were there sociopsychological factors at work which intruded consciously or subsconsciously to vitiate against the English bringing the African into the various levels of colonial society?

Relatively little is known of the reactions of either the English or the African in the first years of encounter. Obviously more evidence is available for an understanding of English actions in the period following the first boatload of black men and women into Virginia. It is highly possible that some Africans learned to read and write in those early years, but their observations and feelings are not known. Only the English record exists and even here the facts are very meager and spotty. It can be surmised that both groups found the habits and practices of the other strange, grating, and foreboding. It is most unfortunate that, at this point it is impossible to analyze the way in which the African responded to the English and their circumstances. Even the tribal community or geographic origins of the early Africans are obscured by the loss of printed materials. More important, to what extent did their reactions spur the English into defensive behavior?

Census figures in the first several decades reveal that by numbers alone the Africans posed no threat. Several censuses taken in the mid-1620s show a very small number of persons of African descent, a situation which prevailed until the 1640s. In 1624 and 1625 a total of twenty persons were counted as being "negars" or "Negors."[1] A handful of blacks arrived in Virginia annually thereafter, principally from Africa but apparently from the Caribbean region as well. Natural increase added to the slowly growing black population. By the latter decades of the seventeenth century, Africans may have constituted approximately five percent of the population. However, there is no certainty as to the number of blacks in the colony. There is some evidence that there were 300 Negroes in 1649. And in Governor William Berkeley's census of 1671, out of a total population of 45,000, 6,000 white servants and 2,000 blacks were listed. Wesley Frank Craven wrote that "the size of Virginia's Negro population at any time after 1625 remains a difficult question."[2]

Regardless of the accuracy of the figures, it is clear that numerically the African constituted a small portion of the colony. Their eventual enslavement was not then the result of overwhelming numbers but of what their presence conveyed to the colonists.

Blacks in the flesh or as representatives of a culture were not unfamiliar to the English prior to colonization. Exploration and trade voyages produced published accounts, geographies, and tales about West Coast Africans in the mid-sixteenth century. These reports were a mixture of fact and fiction, a blending of the ancient classicial writers such as Pliny and Herodotus with contemporary works such as Richard Hakluyt's *Principal Navigations* and John Leo Africanus's *History and Description of Africa.* In addition, there were a substantial number of Africans in London. From the early voyages of the 1550s the practice of bringing blacks into the country became fairly common. In the second half of the century, their numbers grew consistently. By 1601 Queen Elizabeth, "discontented at the great number of 'Negars and blackamoors' which are crept into the realm," issued a proclamation for their transportation out of the country. Significantly, Elizabeth appointed a merchant of Lubeck to remove them from the country.

As eyewitness and geographical reports were published and circulated, a more accurate picture of Africa and its inhabitants emerged and made its way into the literature and drama of the period. Playwrights and novelists used the African figure in both tragedies and comedies in varying ways. Two main male characters, called Moors or "black Moors," developed on the stage. The first was the villainous Moor whose blackness was emphasized in the text; the other a "white" or "tawny Moor" whose skin color was underemphasized. Despite their apparent disparity, the two figures shared in common a blackness and a cruelty indigenous to all Moors. Moreover, the continent itself was used as the setting for a number of plays or as the homeland of many of their characters. The stereotype of the African with a weakness of character is evident in most of the plays of the time. The female Moor also developed along two main lines: a sexual figure used primarily for decoration in her natural environment and her opposite, a sexual, untrustworthy servant in exile.

Regardless of the setting or plot, Africans were heavily utilized in the theatre during the Elizabethan period and beyond. As a source of images, the African served many purposes. Writers who never used the African in their plays nevertheless "referred to the gold of Barbary or to the tears of the crocodile, the monsters of Africa, the horses of Barbary, or merely used the terms Moor, Negro or Ethiop in a simile of blackness, cruelty, jealousy, lustfulness or some other quality commonly credited to Africans."[3]

Skin color was an important form of identification in Elizabethan England. The *blackness* of the African was highlighted in literature. Because it represented the opposite of the Elizabethan ideal of female beauty with its emphasis upon pale, white skin, red lips and cheeks, and light hair— symbolized in contemporary American culture by such cinema figures as Marilyn Monroe and Doris Day, two models who were intended to portray sexuality and innocence respectively—blackness was used to portray its antithesis. Blackness was extensively described in Samuel Johnson's *Dictionary*, the first such English compilation, in the eighteenth century:

BLACK, adj.

1. Of the colour of night.
   In the twilight in the evening, in the *black* and dark night.

   Prov. vii.9

2. Dark.
   The heaven was *black* with clouds and wind, and there was a great rain.

   I Kings, xviii, 45

3. Cloudy of countenance; sullen.
   She has abated me of half my train; Look'd *black* upon me.

   Shakespeare, *King Lear*

4. Horrible; wicked; atrocious.
   Either my country never must be freed, Or I consenting to do *black* a deed.

   Dryden's *Indian Emp.*

5. Dismal; mournful.
   A dire induction am I witness to; And will to France, hoping, the consequence, Will prove as bitter, *black*, and tragical.

   Shakespeare, *Richard III*

6. *Black and Blue.* The color of a brute; a stripe.
   Mistress Ford, good heart, is beaten *black and blue*, that you cannot see a white spot about her.

   *Merry Wives of Windsor*
   And, wing'd with speed and fury, flew To rescue knight from *black and blue*.

   *Hudibras*, cant. ii

The term Black was coupled to extend its descriptive range in phrases such as *"Black-browed"*: "Having black eyebrows; gloomy; dismal; threatening"; and *"Black-guard"*: "A cant word amongst the vulgar; by which is implied a dirty fellow; of the meanest kind"; *"Black-mail"*: "A certain rate of money, corn, cattle, or other consideration, paid to men allied with robbers, to be by them protected from the danger usually rob or steal."[4]

Thus, in Elizabethan England, as Winthrop Jordan in his *White Over Black: American Attitudes Toward the Negro* has demonstrated, "perhaps more than in southern Europe, the concept of blackness was loaded with intense meaning. Long before they found that some men were black, Englishmen found in the idea of blackness a way of expressing some of their most ingrained values. No other color except white conveyed so much emotional impact."[5]

## Denying the African his Name

Attitudinally ingrained with a harsh image of blackness, and having either experienced contact with Africans or read of their behavior in Africa or England, the settlers in North America met the Africans coming off the slave ships with jaundiced views. They were of a different color, of a strange culture and language, possessing divergent views of the diety, and in a servile position. Clearly they were heathens, unblessed and ignorant. More, their names were generally unintelligible and for the most part incomprehensible. They were thus human beings with definite, recognizable flaws, without a clearly defined personality, carriers of foreign ideas and idolatrous practices, not unknown but unknowable in the fullest sense and without substance as defined by English values and customs.

Within this context, the English proceeded to make the African more comprehensible individually and collectively. The process, involving personal, legalistic, religious, economic, and educative complexities, first involved conveying personal names upon the Africans. One of the first options open to the English, who were in the superior position of establishing the terms upon which the two cultures could meet, was the giving of names; familar, Christian names *(Alternative 1: Total Assimilation* and *Alternative 2: Degrees of Unfreedom).*

"The beginning of all instruction," wrote Antithenes in the fifth century B.C., "is the study of names." The power of naming another individual involves a person's self-identification as well as projection of hopes and aspirations. At the same time, it is one of the most powerful forms of social control. The practice of giving and accepting names is universal, existing in all cultures and possessing secular and magical aspects. To the ancient Egyptians, for example, one of the eight parts which made up a man was his name, without which both the man and his afterlife would be destroyed. Indian tribes in the North American continent and cultures in Tibet believed that sickness was the consequence of a name that did not fit the person—"an ill wound is cured, not an ill name," noted George Herbert in *Outlandish Proverbs* in 1640—and that the cure would result only upon the designation of a new name that did fit. The relationship between the Church and naming commenced very early. To symbolize their conversion, the early Christians assumed a new name at the baptismal ceremony, the new name being designated as the "Christianed" or "baptismal" name; the phrase "Christian name" apparently derived from the outdated "Christened name." The early Church recognized the mystical strength of a name by declaring that only the names of martyrs and saints were acceptable at the baptismal ceremony. At the Council of Nicaea in 325 A.D., the Church further enunciated that the names of heathen gods were prohibited as given names. Centuries later, the Church of England also forbade the naming of children after those of heathen origin.[6]

The bestowal of names upon African slaves began immediately after their sale. Africans were given Christian or "practical" names, the latter names stemming from the English difficulty in pronouncing African words. Edward Manning of the slave ship *Thomas Watson* described the solution to this problem in 1860:

> I suppose that all had names in their own dialect, but the effort required to pronounce them was too much for us, so we picked out our favorites and dubbed them 'Main-stay', 'Cat-head', 'Bull's-eye', 'Rope-yarn', and various other sea phrases.[7]

Ship captains, as well as slave traders, listed basic facts, noting physical features, estimation of age, sex, and other related items. "In consideration whereof the said John Skinner covenanted and bargained to deliver unto the said Leonard Calvert, fourteene negro men-slaves, and three women slaves, of betweene 16 and 26 yeare old able and sound in body and limbs . . ." was the brief description of a typical contract of sale in 1642 (see Document 18). Africans were regarded as articles of merchandise and listed as such. Orders to Captain Marmaduke Goodhand in London in 1685 directed him to traders "who will see you paid well for the Freight of the Negroes, as for what will be due for the care of them during their being aboard."[8] Death in mid-passage brought the listing of numbers and/or statements of anonymity, as a "neagerman dep'ted this life whoe died suddenly." Even compassionate descriptions were made within the context of namelessness. "Let it be observed," wrote Captain John Newton in his *Journal of a Slave Trader, 1750-1754* of conditions aboard ship, "that the poor creatures, thus cramped for want of room, are likewise in irons, for the most part both hands and feet, and two together, which makes it difficult for them to turn or move. . . . Dire is the tossing, deep the groans. . . ."[9]

When a semblance of naming occurred, it revealed a sardonic attitude. James Arnold, the surgeon on the English slaver *The Ruby*, wrote in 1787: "The first slave that was traded for, after the brig anchored at the Island of Bimbe, was a girl of about fifteen who was promptly named Eve, for it was usual on slave ships to give the names of Adam and Eve to the first man and woman brought on board."[10]

Permanent naming, however, did not begin until the African's arrival and establishment within the community. It was at this juncture that options were open to the English settlers, options which would disclose predilections. Of the initial group of Africans brought into Jamestown in 1619, only eleven of the names are known and these indicate antecedent Spanish baptism. These included "Anthony," "Frances," "Fernando," "Madelina," "Bastiaen," "Paulo" and "Isabella." Thus over half of the first Africans to disembark in Virginia had already undergone a significant name change, indicating that the practice was indigenous to the slave process. One historian has argued that there exists "a strong possibility that the majority of slaves brought into the Colonies before 1700 had Spanish names."[11]

Whereas many Africans who entered the colonies in the early decades of the seventeenth century had Spanish or Portugese names, children born in the next generation had distinctly English appellations. This striking change can be observed in the case of a child born to Anthony and Isabella, both of African extraction. His name was "William" and while his baptism is recorded, no mention is made of his parents, probably because they had already received the sacraments.[12] This distinction between the first two generations is more apparent in the inventory of 1644: "one negroe man called Anthonio . . . One negroe woman called Mitchaell (Michaela) . . . One negroe woman, Couchaxello . . . One negroe woman, Palassa . . . One negroe girle Mary 4 years old . . . One negroe called Eliz: 3 yeares old." Apparently the adult names derived from the Spanish, the children's from the English.[13]

It is highly conceivable that at this early date, the English settlers attempted to create an African in his image by changing the names of those with Spanish designations *(Alternative 1)*. Among the names of the first boatload of Africans were two Johns, a William, an Edward, and a Margarett, whose names may have been anglicized from Juan, Guillen, Eduardo, and Margarita.[14] Some names were clearly binational, as illustrated by an African called "John Pedro." Clearly, what emerges is a deep-seated reluctance on the part of the English to accommodate to Spanish and African names.

Two censuses taken in Virginia in the 1620s further reveal the denial of African designations. The census of 1624 lists twenty-two living blacks in the colony and one as having died in the previous year. "What is most striking about the appearance of these blacks in the census is that although most of them had been in America for five years, none is accorded a last name and almost half are recorded with no name at all." Entries of Africans in the census were written as "one negar," "a Negors Woman" or just "negors." A comparison with Caucasians in the census is striking. Few of the latter had incomplete names, and where parts were missing other information was provided, such as "Symon, an Italien."[15] Thus, negative distinctions are conveyed in the census in 1624.

The following year another tabulation of the colony was taken, this one more exacting and complete. Twenty-three blacks were listed, and again, the information given was extremely scanty in contrast with whites. Some given names are listed and only one possessed a full name: John Pedro. Equally important in both censuses was the information listed with the names. Conspicuously missing from the rolls of the blacks were many items such as age, date of arrival, ship of passage, possessions, food staples and livestock, statistics which appeared alongside names of white inhabitants. Moreover, despite their having been in the colony for six years, none of the Africans was mentioned as being free. All were either "specifically listed under heading of 'servants' or were included in the holdings of free white men who held white as well as black 'servants.'" Significantly, the placing of blacks at the end of the lists of servants, occasionally together with that of an Indian, suggests a distinct status of inferiority.[16]

The omission of family names for blacks in the censuses of the 1620s was a common practice throughout the century. This was partly due to the fact that only a handful of Africans were accorded surnames: "Andrew Moore," "Philip Gowen," "Robert Trayes," "John Phillip," "Bostian Ken," "Zippora Potter," and several others had totally Anglican names. Rather, most blacks were designated by their skin color, status, or relation to owner. Court records are replete with such phrases. In 1672, a suit was brought against "Betty Negro" for insulting a son and his mother; a "Wonn Negro" testified in a witchcraft case in 1679 and a "Mary Black" was tried, convicted, and imprisoned for witchcraft in 1692 but petitioned and was released the following year. But more often, either a single name or a name followed by a descriptive phrase was used to describe blacks. "Hannah" was convicted of stealing and later acquitted (1679); "Jugg" was whipped for fornication

(1660), as were "Grace" and "Juniper" (1674); "a Mulata named Manuel" was listed in another case. "Mingo the Negro" was a witness in a suit involving warehouse arson (1680); there was a case involving John Barnes's "neager maide servant" (1653). "Whereas Will a Runaway Negroe Suspected to have Lett out of Prison a Negroe Condemned the last Court and Confesseth that he did See the Negroe breake Loose out of irons . . . " (1673); "Angell a negro Servant . . . " sued for her freedom (1673).[17] Not all cases contained abbreviated names or names-and-descriptions. Occasionally there were full names such as "a negro named John Punch," who in a decision in 1640 was ordered by the court "to serve his said master or his assigns for the time of his natural Life here or elsewhere."[18]

Spanish and English names, then, took the place of African designations in the seventeenth century. Significantly, in all of the inventories of the era, only a few names suggesting an African past appeared: "Samba," "Mookinga" and "Palassa." Gone on the books, at least, was any hint—other than the word "slave" or "servant" or a variation of the term "Negro"—that a portion of the population was of African origin. By the last half of the century, the term "slave" would come to define the African but the name which accompanied that status was usually western European.

## Renaming in the English Image

It was at this point that the English made a concerted attempt to create an African partly in his own image within the matrixes of religious and cultural forces *(Alternative 2)*. Consequently it is not surprising that the majority of the names given to the African derive from Biblical, historical or whimsical sources. But the process apparently had its limits. While many owners did not complain of slaves taking their surnames, some were piqued by the usage of their full names for a black person. Cotton Mather, the sensitive Puritan leader, was incensed when he learned that a slave had been named after him:

> A Lieutenant of a Man of War whom I am a Stranger to, designing to putt an Indignity upon me, has called his *Negro-Slave* by the Name of COTTON-MATHER.

Samuel Sewall wrote in his diary of Mather's actions:

> Mr. Cotton Mather came to Mr. Wilkin's shop and there talked very sharply against me as if I used his father worse than a Negar; spake so loud that the people in the street might hear him.[19]

In the earliest and subsequent encounters with the African, then, the English made little attempt to learn the names of their captives and workers and thus severely restricted the African's sense of identity and their own understanding. It can be argued that captives, by their very servile and demeaned position, lose a considerable amount of identity in the overall process of being passed from one party to another. But in the encapsulated environment of the seventeenth century, in the tight quarters of the community in Maryland and Virginia, the English must have been informed by many Africans of their names by the usual means of physical communications when the parties are of different cultures. That the English largely refused to heed this basic sense of self attested to their general denial of the African as an equal. This type of denial is clearly not unique to the English settler of the seventeenth century. But a significant option was open at a time when cultural interaction was occurring, a time when the English were in the process of defining their position vis-à-vis the African. The failure to view the Africans in their own context seriously affected the African's ultimate standing in the community.

By contrast, the English were relatively open to, if not intrigued by, various aspects of Indian culture and made concerted attempts to learn Indian designations. They were, after all, the outsiders in a strange environment. Survival depended upon learning all of the pitfalls as well as the advantages of the terrain. But the interaction occurred for other reasons as well, not the least of which was the English recognition of Indian strengths. As George Axtell cogently understood, "The shifting frontier between wilderness and civilization seems an unlikely place for a school, but the cultures that meet there never fail to educate each other."[20]

In reports, diaries, and letters the English spelled and translated Indian names, places, tribes, crops and other important items. The spellings of these words varied according to the author—John Rolfe listed his wife's name as "Pokahuntas"—but the important thing is that Indian language was acknowledged, sometimes adopted, and communicated to others by the English. Indian leaders' names, such as "Powhatan" or "Pohatan," "Opechancanough" and others, appear with regularity in the dispatches of John Smith and other English writers. Smith writes of the rivers "Wighcocomoco" and "Kusharawaocke." Difficult tribe names are recorded in the *Records of the Virginia Company:* "Quiyoughquohanocks," "Chickokonini"; and by Smith in his writings: "Soraphanigh," "Nause," "Arsek," "Nautaquake." Ralph Hamor, secretary to the colony, wrote in 1615 in *A True Discourse of the Present State of Virginia* of meeting with a group of Indians "who walked up and down, by us and amongst us, the best of them inquiring for our Weroance or king ... "[21] If the English made a similar serious effort to learn African designations, the record does not show it.

That attempts were made by the Africans to retain continuity with the past, however, is clear; but their efforts regarding names were only partially successful. Still, personal struggles were unceasing. Paul Cuffee, the dynamic shipping merchant of early nineteenth-century Massachusetts, was one of the few blacks who managed to replace his surname, "Slocum," which derived from his former owner. In 1778 he selected the name "Cuffee" after his father's day-name, which in West Africa means "male born on Friday." It was an African practice to name their children after days of the week; and "Cuffee" was perhaps one of the most common of the day-names in the country.[22]

Alex Haley's intensive activities in the mid-twentieth century are a unique example of an individual's search for geneological origins. Haley's "furtherest-back-person"—his Kinte clan blood relation who was captured while chopping wood near his village in West Africa in 1767 and enslaved in Virginia—was named "Toby" by his white master. When other slaves called him by that name, he protested, repeating over and again that his name was "Kin-tay." In fact, his name was "Kunta" and he descended from the Kinte clan in the Gambian region. Undeterred by efforts to eliminate his past, Kunta repeated not only his name but also vital facts of his background to "Kizzy," his daughter:

> As she grew up her African daddy often showed her different things, telling her what they were in his native tongue. Pointing at a banjo, for example, the African uttered, 'ko'; or pointing at a river near the plantation, he would say, 'Kamby Bolong.' Many of his strange words started with a 'k' sound, and the little, growing Kizzy learned gradually that they identified different things.[23]

Kizzy retained the information and passed it on to her children so that it became part of the folk history of the Haley family. In sessions after dinner, members of the family would sit around talking about their history:

> The furtherest-back-person Grandma and the others talked of—always in tones of awe, I noticed—they would call 'The African.' They said that some ship brought him to a place that they pronounced 'Naplis.' They said that some 'Mas' John Waller' bought him for his plantation in 'Spotsylvania County, Va.' This African kept on escaping, the fourth time trying to kill the 'hateful po' cracker' slave-catcher, who gave him the punishment of castration or of losing one foot. This African took a foot being chopped off with an ax against a tree stump, they said, and he was about to die. But his life was saved by 'Mas' John's' brother—'Mas' William Waller', a doctor, who was so furious about what had happened that he bought the African for himself and gave him the name of 'Toby.'[24]

Two centuries after his great-great-great-great grandfather had been captured, Haley, who had collaborated in the writing of *The Autobiography of Malcolm X*, was able to retrace his ancestry on the basis of those meager African words, sounds, and bits of history. The personal voyage was made possible by the furious inner demands of an African who refused to concede his name.

## The Impact of Namelessness

Kunta was obviously not alone in his desire to preserve a sense of identity. Though largely unsuccessful in the colonies in the seventeenth century, some later Africans who served as slaves managed to protect their appellations. Ayuba Suleiman Ibrahima Diallo of Bondu, a merchant who served as slave for two years in Maryland in the 1730s but eventually made his way back to his native land after being emancipated and brought to England, was given the slave name of "Simon." He discarded this name in favor of Job Ben Solomon, the Biblical title being the English equivalent of Ayuba.[25]

The significance of a name as a sign of self was recognized by the Black Muslims in the mid-twentieth century. Rejecting their Anglicized names but unable to pinpoint their African heritage, they took the letter "X" as a symbol of a broken past and new dignity. One of the most influential Muslims, Malcolm X, argued vehemently for a "knowledge of history" as a prerequisite of political power and a sense of separate ethnic identities:

I would like to point out . . . that I wasn't born Malcolm Little. Little is the name of the slave master who owned one of my grandparents during slavery, a white man, and the name Little was handed down to my grandfather, to my father and to me. But after hearing the teachings of the Honorable Elijah Muhammad and realizing that Little is an English name, and I'm not an Englishman, I gave the Englishman back his name; and since my own had been stripped from me, hidden from me, and I don't know it, I use X . . .[26]

Stripped of name and status and generally unable to communicate—and particularly to *defend*—their culture, the Africans found themselves in an extremely vulnerable position, virtually dependent upon the motivations of their superiors. The Africans' weakness was not only the consequence of being a captive but also of the nature of their captivity. Previous titles, positions, family, background, or skills meant little if economic demands required brawn and durability. Sometimes the name played ironic against the backdrop of slavery. Olaudah Equiano, who was kidnapped as a boy in the 1750s, bought his freedom, wrote his memoirs and was active in the British antislavery movement, noted the significance of his name: "I was named Olaudah, which, in our language signifies vicissitude, or fortune also; one favoured, and having a loud voice, and well spoken" (see Document 19).[27]

African names derived from varied sources: days of the week or months of the year; relations to divinations and/or religious events; to seasonal or episodic changes; and to ancestral backgrounds. The tribe of which Ayuba Suleiman was a member designated their names after ancestors, including the names of several previous generations, but they further used surnames in the Western style. In Olaudah's clan, "our children were named after some event, some circumstance, or fancied foredoing at the time of their birth."[28]

However, these complexities were generally ignored or denied by the colonists in the seventeenth century. In their place a simplified system of single appellations of Christian and Anglican roots was instituted. Africans with Spanish names had these names retained or changed to comport with the English. What the English settlers created was a class of incomplete people, without family names, devoid of cultural connections, and indefensible.

Yet, it might be argued that the English were hoping to lessen the gap of unfamiliarity by giving the new people familiar names which would ally them or incorporate them into colonial life. Many living things, after all, were given English names by the colonists, including pets and farm animals. But even granting paternalistic motives, depriving the Africans an important aspect of their identity was belittling if not infantalizing.

The general denial of the Africans' original names served further to enhance English ethnocentrism—for to name a person is to have considerable power over that individual. In this instance, the option of permitting the African his own identity was apparently unexercised, thereby exacerbating a sense of superiority and haughtiness. Already degraded by being taken captive, the Africans were further undercut by the inability to project their own selves. Being baptized and receiving an English or Spanish name placed them in a position similar to that of the powerless child. Obviously, this is not to say that they were children but to argue that in the eyes of those who had the authority to designate such actions, they were in a similar position.

## Notes

1. Alden T. Vaughan, "Blacks in Virginia: A Note on the First Decade," *William and Mary Quarterly*, 3rd ser., vol. 39 (July, 1972), pp. 471-73.

2. Wesley Frank Craven, *White, Red, and Black: The Seventeenth-Century Virginian* (Charlottesville: University Press of Virginia, 1971), p. 98.

3. Eldred Jones, *Othello's Countrymen: The African in English Renaissance Drama* (Oxford: Oxford University Press, 1965), p. 126.

4. Samuel Johnson, *A Dictionary of the English Language* (London: 1805), vol. 1.

5. Winthrop D. Jordan, *White Over Black: American Attitudes Towards the Negro, 1550-1812* (Chapel Hill, N.C.: University of North Carolina Press, 1968), p. 7.

6. Elsdon C. Smith, *The Story of Our Names* (New York: Harper & Row, 1950, ch. 1.

7. George Francis Dow, ed., *Slave Ships and Slaving* (Port Washington, N.Y.: Kennikat Press, 1927, reprint ed., 1969), p. 295.

8. Elizabeth Donnan, ed., *Documents Illustrative of the History of the Slave Trade to America* (New York: Octagon Books, 1969), vol. 4, p. 11.

9. Newbell Niles Puckett, "Names of American Negro Slaves," in *Studies in the Science of Sociology*, ed. G.P. Murdock (New Haven, Conn.: Yale University Press, 1937), p. 473; Bernard Martin and Mark Spurrell, eds., *The Journal of a Slave Trader: John Newton, 1750-1754* (London: Epworth Press, 1962), p. 110.

10. Dow, *Slave Ships and Slaving*, p. 172.

11. Murray Heller, ed., *Black Names in America: Origins and Usage, Collected by Newbell Niles Puckett* (Boston: G.K. Hall, 1974). This is an exaggeration, for many Africans went unnamed in the official censuses of the period and others are missing.

12. Helen T. Catterall, *Judicial Cases Concerning American Slavery and the Negro* (New York: Octagon Books, 1968), vol. 1, pp. 55-56.

13. Ibid., p. 56.

14. Ibid.

15. Vaughan, "Blacks in Virginia," p. 472.

16. Ibid., pp. 471-75.

17. Robert C. Twombley and Richard H. Moore, "Black Puritan: The Negro in Seventeenth Century Massachusetts," *William and Mary Quarterly*, 3rd ser., vol. 24 (April, 1967), pp. 224-42; Catterall, *Judicial Cases Concerning Slavery*, pp. 76-81.

18. Catterall, *Judicial Cases Concerning Slavery*, p. 77.

19. Twombley and Moore, "Black Puritan," p. 226.

20. George Axtell, "The Scholastic Philosophy of the Wilderness," *William and Mary Quarterly*, 3rd ser., vol. 29 (July, 1972), p. 336.

21. Ralph Hamor, *A True Discourse of the Present State of Virginia, and the Successe of the Affaires there till 18 of June 1614* (London: John Beale, 1615), p. 97.

22. J.L. Willard, "The West African Day-Names in Nova Scotia," *Names*, vol. 19 (September, 1971), p. 259; see also Henry M. Sherwood, "Paul Cuffee," *Journal of Negro History*, vol. 8 (1923), pp. 153-232; Katherine A. Wilder, "Captain Paul Cuffee, Master Mariner of Westport, Massachusetts, 1759-1817," *The Bulletin of the Society for the Preservation of New England Antiquities*, vol. 63 (Winter, 1973), p. 78; and Sheldon H. Harris, *Paul Cuffee: Black American and the African Return* (New York: Simon and Schuster, 1972). There is contradictory evidence regarding the change of the Cuffee name. Wilder indicates that Paul changed the family name in 1778. However, there is an 1854 letter in Harris's work by Cuffee's daughter, Ruth, who noted that the name change occurred when Cuffee Slocum was granted freedom by his master. According to her version, owner Captain Ebenezer Slocum "would not have . . . Cuffee's children to go by the name of Slocum. So they called them by their father's name, Cuffee" (p. 264).

23. Alex Haley, "My Furtherest-Back-Person—'The African'," *New York Times Magazine*, July 16, 1972, p. 13.

24. Ibid.

25. Philip D. Curtin, "Ayuba Suleiman Diallo of Bondu," in *Africa Remembered*, ed. Philip Curtin (Madison: University of Wisconsin Press, 1967), p. 37, n. 27.

26. In a debate with James Farmer, then director of the Congress of Racial Equality. See also *The Autobiography of Malcolm X* (New York: Grove Press, 1964), p. 201: "The Muslim's 'X' symbolized the true African family name that he never could know. For me, my 'X' replaced the white slavemaster name of 'Little' which some blue-eyed devil named Little had imposed upon my paternal forebearers. The receipt of my 'X' meant that forever after in the nation of Islam, I would be known as Malcolm X."

27. G.I. Jones, "Olaudah Equiano of the Niger Ibo," in *Africa Remembered*, ed. Philip Curtin, p. 79.

28. Ibid., pp. 35, 79.

# 4

# The Decisions, The Laws

"Bee it Enacted . . . "
Negro Angell v. Matthews, McIlwaine 413, (1675):
"Angell a negro Servant to Capt Matthews deced Petitioning to this Court that her Said master promised that when he died shee should be free which being Examined, It is ordered that she Returne to her Service."
Catterall, *Judicial Cases Concerning Slavery*

## Judicial Decisions: Towards a Legal Status as Slave

Laws reflect the customs, concerns, and intentions of a people. Devised to clarify issues and solve problems, the juridical process acts as an inhibitor of choices, but also as a definer of allowable choices, and is designed to direct behavior towards socially acceptable ends. Laws are the inheritors of the immediate past and mirror the expectations of a future unencumbered. They are, in short, a reflection of the anxieties and objectives of groups who desire to use the law to maintain control over actions and thus are a tangible guide into the workings of a society.

Although the first Africans in the Virginia and Maryland colonies were legally amphorous, sandwiched somewhere within the status of servitude, they were in an extremely vulnerable position. Given their indefinite legal place—for having no indenture they could not easily be regarded in the same category as whites—Africans wound up at various levels of society. While some blacks became permanent workers *(Alternative 3: Lifetime Slavery)*, others were given their freedom after years of servitude, in the manner of indentured servants *(Alternative 2)*. This situation would generally prevail until the legislation of the 1660s removed any doubts as to the place of Africans in the colonies *(Alternative 4: Perpetual Slavery)*.

Court cases in the 1620s thus made no distinction between white and black servants. In that first decade, however, distinctions of other types were being made which would result in specific decisions and laws. For it appears that from the very beginning, as illustrated by names, census data, and other evidence, blacks were in "a singularly debased status in the eyes of white Virginians. If not subjected to permanent and inheritable bondage during that decade . . . black Virginians were at least on their way to such a condition."[1]

Not more than eleven years after the arrival of the boatload of Africans, there appeared the first of a series of cases which involved and seriously impaired the condition of blacks. The circumstances surrounding the case of Hugh Davis is unknown but the decision is chillingly clear. The General Court ordered that "Hugh Davis to be soundly whipped, before an assembly of Negroes and others for abusing himself to the dishonor of God and shame of Christians, by defiling his body in lying with a negro; which fault he is to acknowledge next Sabbath day."[2] Just why Davis was brought before the court and adjudged guilty for having physical relations with a black person is a matter of conjecture. The court record does not indicate the *name* or the *sex* of the individual. Regardless, concern in this area is evident from other cases which were brought before the court. A decade later Robert Sweet was hauled before the magistrates. In this 1640 decision, it was held that "Robert Sweet to do penance in church according to laws of England, for getting a negroe woman with child and the woman whipt."[3] Again, the woman is not named, nor is the status of either person disclosed.

Sexual restrictions were not the only concern of white Virginians. Despite the community regulation which involved all able-bodied males serving in the militia and carrying arms, by the close of the 1630s blacks were specifically prohibited from participating. "All persons," the General Council ruled in 1639, "except negroes [are] to be provided with arms and ammunition or be fined at pleasure of the Governor and Council."[4] Denying blacks from bearing arms while permitting white servants to do so, despite the small numbers of the former in the colony, was a mark of differentiation revealing either an anxiety or an evolving distinct status as a laborer. In Virginia and then in Maryland in 1648, laws which prohibited blacks from bearing arms specifically permitted white servants to carry weapons.

That blacks were being conceived in different labor terms could be seen in a series of cases which appeared before the court in the early 1640s, a time when blacks constituted less than 2.5 percent of the population, three hundred souls out of approximately fifteen thousand. The majority of these individuals had been imported into the colony in the preceding decade. Whether the increase in their numbers exacerbated the need to define the status of blacks in general is hard to ascertain. What is clear is the substantial number of cases before the court which dealt with the problem of placing the black man and woman within the social structure.

In July, 1640, three servants who had run away were apprehended in Maryland and stood trial. All three were given "the punishment of whipping and to have thirty stripes apiece." Two of the group, a man named "Victory, a dutchman" and a Scotsman, James Gregory, were specifically given an additional term of one year to their indenture and upon expiration of that sentence "to serve the colony for three whole years." But the third party was a black man. John Punch was ordered to serve "his said master or his assigns for the time of his natural Life here or elsewhere."[5] Three months later an escape plot by six white servants of Captain William Pierce and "a Negro of Mr. Reginalds" ended when the group was apprehended in the Elizabeth River on a skiff carrying corn, powder, and guns belonging to Captain Pierce. In the complaint brought before the court by their owner, it is significant that the black, a man named Emanuel, is not listed as a servant; apparently he was already a laborer for life. The person who directed the plot was Miller, a white man. For his initiative Miller was severely punished; he was given thirty stripes, ordered to wear shackles on his legs for one year and possibly longer, had an additional seven years service to the colony at the conclusion of his indenture, and had the letter "R" burned into his cheek. The letter stood for "Rogue." The other whites received less harsh treatment, but none got away with less than two years added to their service. "Emanuel the Negro," on the other hand, was given virtually all of the punishments meted out to Miller save for the additional service. Apparently this stipulation was unnecessary as the terms of his limitless work were comprehended by all involved.[6]

A year later, in a case involving the status of a black child, the position of the nonwhite population was further restricted. John Graweere was a servant who brought suit before the General Court for the possession of his daughter, the offspring of a union with "a negro woman belonging to Lieut. Robert Sheppard." Graweere apparently purchased the child with funds derived from his work, an arrangement he had with his master William Evans. Graweere related to the court his intentions as a Christian, declaring that he planned to rear his child "in the fear of God and in the knowledge of religion taught and exercised in the church of England." The court ruled in his favor and ordered that the child be free from Evans or his assigns and "to be and remain at the disposing and education of the said Graweere and the child's godfather, who undertaketh to see it brought up in the Christian religion as aforesaid." While the verdict was in a black man's favor, several forces appeared to be operative. In the first instance, no case would have taken place if Graweere had been white; there would have been no question of the ownership of a child under these circumstances. Secondly, "the fact that Sheppard was able to sell the child suggests that as early as 1641 a Negro servant's children were sometimes considered the property of the mother's master and disposable by him. From this single remarkable case it becomes evident that the position of the Negro was deteriorating in Virginia."[7]

Taken together, the cases involving the unnamed runaway servant, Emanuel, and Graweere all point to the condition of slavery for some blacks barely twenty years after their arrival into the colony (Alternative 3). Official acts in the following decade confirm the direction of court decisions of the earlier period. In distinguishing between Indians and others, the General Assembly ruled that Indian children in the households of colonists should not be slaves. On the other hand, a decision before the court was listed in the following manner: "Mulatto held to be a slave and appeal taken."[8]

## The Legal Problem of the Nonwhite Christian

The momentum of the colonists' actions towards using blacks as permanent laborers, however, was often undermined by religious factors. From the very beginning, as illustrated by English perceptions of Indians as heathens and the reactions to this, the settlers were determined to convert the idolatrous. The unsaved, whether Indian or African, received the holy water and were thus converted to the faith. Conversion, it is clear, often brought significant rights and privileges. There is evidence to indicate that those Africans who received the baptismal rite prior to their arrival in Virginia were accorded a higher place within the community as compared to other Africans and gradually ascended from servants to free citizens.[9] Since being a Christian was a mark of freedom, the question of whether a baptized African could be so construed was constantly before the courts.

That baptism was regarded as secularly rewarding was illustrated by a ruling of the General Assembly in a 1642 case involving an Indian. It was declared that he was to be released from lifelong servitude because of his "speaking perfectly the English tongue and desiring baptism."[10] In this particular case, it might be argued that what motivated the assembly was not only the Indian's desire to be admitted to the sacrament but also his educational prowess. It is certain that black Christians within the colony were more highly regarded than non-Christian blacks; black Christians, for example, had the right to bring suit in a court of law.

Conversion to Christianity, then, was an acceptable and, in terms of legal status, a significant option which the English permitted nonwhites (Alternative 2). It was an act which "evidently conferred upon blacks a rank higher than that of a slave" or a bondsman whose term of service was indeterminate.[11] Acceptance of baptism was an important step in the English mind towards the development of civility and rationality. Baptism thus occasionally brought manumission or at least a greater personal flexibility for the black man or woman. Consequently, religious grounds served as the basis for a substantial number of suits.

But even in this area the options were circumscribed. Colonists were troubled by the seeming conflict between "Africanness" and "Christianity," between their attitude towards Africans as being uneducable and as acceptable converts. As several important cases indicate, the question of where a converted African fit into the class structure was perplexing. Three cases highlight the ambiguity of the situation.

In 1644, a baptized man, "a Mulata named Manuel" who had been purchased as a "Slave for Ever" was judged by the General Assembly not to be in that position but "to serve as other Christian servants do" and was ordered to be set free. Thus baptism brought release for Manuel. But there was a catch to the decision: the assembly set the time of his freedom to begin in 1665. Since other Christian servants were not required to serve apprenticeships for such an extended period, the ruling points to conversion as affecting status change but also to the operational forces pulling in the opposite direction. The owner of Manuel, moreover, immediately sought compensation for the loss of a laborer; that he could do so reflected upon blacks as being in service in perpetuity.

A second case involved a man named Fernando who in 1667 argued that he was "a Christian and had been several yeares in England." Fernando offered as evidence of his conversion several papers which the clerk observed were written "in Portugell or some other language which the Court could not understand." Whether or not the court chose to understand or called in an interpreter is unknown. What is recorded is the court's ruling that no cause of action existed and the dismissal of the suit.[12] The third situation was more complicated and involved a black woman, Elizabeth Key, who was born of Thomas Key and an unnamed slave woman. Her case, brought before the court in 1655-56, was based on the grounds of her having had a free father and thus inheriting his condition, as well as her conversion to Christianity. Her period of servitude had elapsed after being sold to another party. Although the jury accepted her plea, her case was appealed by an overseer of an involved estate, and the general court overturned the earlier decision and declared her a slave. The Key case proceded through additional judicial maneuverings, but this case and Fernando's suit indicated that some black laborers were not only being held in lifetime servitude but that their situation also had precedent in law. There may well have been other cases which dealt with the relationship between conversion and legal status but the loss of "great quantities of Virginia's seventeenth-century legal records" over the centuries has only confounded the problem.[13]

## Economic and Legislative Trends towards Slavery

The very fact of such trials strongly suggests the precariousness of the African's standing within the community, a precariousness which was deeply affected by factors inherent in the community at that particular moment. One such factor was the continuing need for a stable labor supply in an expanding market economy, for a body of workers who would not be eager to take off to other territories or be freed after their indenture was fulfilled. There is every indication that either because of the recognition of such a need, or because of other tangible causes already discussed, the colonists began to assess black laborers in higher valuations. In the 1640s and 1650s, in estate inventories and bills of sale, the prices for blacks increased noticeably. This was generally true for children as well as for adult workers. Particularly significant is that black workers were even more highly valued than those white servants who had their full indentures to complete. The increasing estimation of blacks can be seen in colonial inventories. William Burdett's inventory in 1643 listed eight white servants with time to serve at assessments of 400 to 1,100 pounds of tobacco as compared to a black youth—"Caine the negro boy, very Obedient"—and a young girl who were valued at 3,000 and 2,000 pounds respectively, with no indication of remaining service time. Of the seven workers belonging to James Stone in 1648, the two Negroes, Emaniell and Mingo, were not only listed as being worth 2,000 pounds of tobacco apiece, but neither had any terms of service cited after his name; the whites, on the other hand, were valued from 1,300 to 1,500 pounds and all of them had full names and terms of their remaining service specifically listed.

Inventories in the following decade were similar. In the estate of Major Peter Walker, 1655, two men servants with four years remaining in their indenture were recorded as being worth 1,300 pounds of tobacco apiece and a woman servant with two years to go was assessed at 800 pounds, but two black youths with no service term limit were cited at 4,100 pounds each and a black girl was rated at 5,500 pounds. Seasoned white hands with limited work years on other plantations were registered as being worth less than blacks who had no set work term, regardless of age.[14] In the case of the blacks, it is important to note that no years of service were affixed after their names.

Wills and deeding provisions during the same period further demonstrate the condition of some blacks in work perpetuity. Prior to his return to England in 1646, Francis Pott sold a black woman, "Marchant," and a black boy, "Will," to Stephen Charleton for use by him as well as "his heyers etc. forever." Similarly, in 1652, William Whittington sold a ten-year-old black girl named "Jowan" to John Pitt and "his heyers, Exors. Adms. or Assigns"; not only was the girl herself sold but also "her Issue and Produce . . . and their services forever." Other black female servants and their children were also passed down to others in permanent bondage *(Alternative 4).*[15]

In the absence of contracts, blacks frequently labored for unspecified lengths of time *(Alternative 3).* In 1635, Charles Harmer imported eight Negroes to work on his newly acquired two thousand acres, the largest number of blacks secured by a single person in that year. All were listed with English surnames: Evan Joans, Thomas Cole, James Courtney, Lazarus manning (sic), Thomas Davis, Richard wryth (sic), John Symons, Richard newton (sic), Elizabeth Bennett, Rebecca Slaughter, and Mary Chester. Despite economic reverses, some of these same laborers remained in the possession of his widow two decades later.[16] This practice was repeated throughout the colony, its import felt by many other planters.

Legislative enactments reflected and reinforced this trend towards enslavement. Statutes passed in the 1650s contained crucial terminology relating to slavery. In 1655, the Virginia assembly decreed that "if the Indians shall bring in any children as gages of their good and quiet intentions to us and amity with us . . . we will not use them as slaves, but do their best to bring them up in Christianity, civility and the knowledge of necessary trades." The application of the term "slave" would imply that some individuals, excepting Indians, were already conceived of in this category. The wording of a 1659 commercial transaction with the Dutch was quite specific in this sense: " . . . if the said Dutch or other foreigners shall import any negro-slaves . . . " the agreement stated. In 1661, an act entitled "English running away with negroes" made direct reference to the process of permanent bondage.

> That in case any English servant shall run away in company with any negroes who are incapable of making satisfaction by addition of time, bee it enacted that the English so running away in company with them shall serve for the time of the said negroes absence as they are to do for their owne by a former act (Alternative 4: *see Document 20).*

If blacks were "incapable" of providing satisfaction by additional time, it meant that they were already in a state of enslavement and not regarded as servants for a limited period. The following year a more extensive law relating to "Run-aways" was enacted. Repeating the admonition against accompanying fleeing blacks, the statute detailed severe punishments.

Not only was the person who accompanied blacks to "serve the masters of the said negroes for their absence so long as they should have done by this act if they had not been slaves," but in addition, "if the negroes be lost or dye in such time of their being run away, the Christian servants in company with them shall by proportion among them, either pay fower thousand five hundred pounds of tobacco and caske or fower yeares service for every negro soe lost or dead." Such was the buying power of black laborers (see Document 20).

These statutes point up English awareness of ethnic differences, certainly as between Indians and Africans and their status within the colony, but more particularly as between whites and blacks regardless of position. In 1662, a law was passed which gave full expression to racial distinctions, indicating a consciousness that had been developing within the colony for some time. The statute was complex for it dealt with various aspects of white/black behavior and furthered the establishment and perpetuation of slavery within the colony. Troubled about both the numbers and status of children born of white and black persons, the assembly succinctly reversed the traditional view of law that the child inherits the status of the father:

> Whereas some doubts have arrisen whether children got up by an Englishman upon a negro woman should be slave or free, *Be it therefore enacted and declared by this present grand assembly*, that all children borne in this country shall be held bond or free only according to the condition of the mother.

Further, to prevent such sexual unions, the assembly provided punishment of double fines for any "Christian" caught fornicating with "a negro man or woman."[17]

The statute is significant for what it did and did not say. As there is no definition of the term "slave," it can be assumed that the status conveyed a specific interpretation to those involved in the preparation of the ordinance and to the larger colony. Whether the implications of the law were fully understood at the time of its adoption is difficult to ascertain; but it is hard to imagine how, after living and coping with the ambiguities of the blacks' status in society for more than forty years, the assembly did not comprehend its broad objectives. Indeed, having dealt with blacks in relation to many literal activities such as defense, work, sex, taxes, education, religion, and oral situations including those of naming and communicating, the men of the assembly well understood the language and meaning of their actions. By reversing the legal concept of the children inheriting the father's status, the inevitable perpetuation of enslavement for blacks was ensured for their children, whether of black or white ancestry *(Alternative 4)*. The prohibition against sexual intercourse followed a pattern seen in the Hugh Davis and Robert Sweet cases and served notice that colony policy would remain strict in this crucial area. Moreover, in distinguishing between free and unfree blacks, there could be no denying the existence of an accepted and structured form of slavery.

While the act did not in itself establish slavery, it immeasurably narrowed the options for whites in devising policies for working out their relationship with blacks. This relationship was even more constricted five years later. One of the viable means by which blacks could secure their freedom was through an act of conversion. But in 1667 this mechanism was eliminated. Apparently, concern about the freeing of black Christians, especially children born into the colony, had been felt and acted upon. It is interesting to note that in recognizing the problem, the assembly explicitly took cognizance of a body of children who were already "slaves by birth" and then proceeded to specify their future status as well as the position of all blacks who had been baptized. "Whereas some doubts have risen," the assembly laconically observed,

> whether children that are slaves by birth, and by the charity and piety of their owners made partakers of the blessed sacrament of baptisme, should by vertue of their baptisme be made free; *It is enacted* . . . that the conferring of baptisme doth not alter the condition of the person as to his bondage or freedom;

With that avenue virtually closed, the assembly counselled that masters

> may more carefully endeavor the propagation of Christianity by permitting children, though slaves, or those of greater growth if capable, to be admitted to that sacrament.[18]

It is clear that religious considerations were being superceded by other factors. The assembly did not order masters to provide religious instruction—indeed, no punishment was to be given to those owners who kept their slaves in a state of heathenism—and grounded their reasoning on the intellectual and spiritual limitations of blacks. Redemption was to occur only in a state of bondage.

Laws in the late 1660s and 1670s similarly expressed slavery as the condition for blacks and further separated blacks and whites. An ordinance in 1669 exonerated white masters from a felony charge if they killed a slave who was resisting not only the master but "other[s] by his masters orders correcting him (see Document 21). The distinction between the terms "servant" and "slave" comes through clearly in the same year in a series of detailed acts dealing with runaways. Directed towards servants, the statute also subjected slaves to the same penalties: " . . . that the servant not being slave (who are also comprehended in this act) . . . " Black women were differentiated from whites. In the previous year, the assembly pondered the question of whether Negro women who had been set free were exempt from tithing. Though the assembly did make them liable for payment of taxes, it also took the occasion to observe that such women, despite their free status, "yet ought not in all respects to be admitted to a full fruition of the exemptions and impunities of the English." Differentiations appeared in still other actions. Addressing themselves to the problem of time to be served by Indians captured in battle and then sold to the English, it was ruled that "all servants not being christians imported into this colony by shipping shall be slaves for their lives." But the act recognized another group, for it distinguished between place of origin. Non-Christians who came into the colony "by land shall serve, if boyes or girles, untill thirty yeares of age, if men or women twelve yeares and no longer." The act clearly upgraded the Indian who was obviously indigenous to the land and discriminated against the African who was brought in by ship. Though it was still possible for Africans who had undergone conversion prior to disembarking to argue in favor of their being servants, it almost always took legal action to be classified in that rank.[19]

Official descriptions of the time also acknowledged the differences between race and status. The Lords Commissions in England submitted an "Enquiries to the Governor of Virginia" in 1670, to which Governor William Berkeley replied the following year. To the question, "What number of planters, servants and slaves ...?" Berkeley was quite specific. "We suppose," he wrote, "and I am very sure we do not much miscount, that there is in Virginia above forty thousand persons, men, women and children, and of which there are two thousand *black slaves*, six thousand *christian servants* ... "[20]

## Narrowing Options for Freedom

Yet, even while an equation was being legally hammered out whereby servant was construed as white and slave was known to be black, the various options which had been used by the English to permit blacks to join the community as free individuals were maintained *(Alternative 1)*. The contradictory nature of the situation persisted well into the 1670s. Though many black children and adults were treated as and called slaves, a small number did receive their freedom after a period of labor. A limited free black population developed throughout the century, their numbers increasing and their status becoming more defined. The avenues by which blacks could become part of the free classes at this time were varied. Limited terms of service were uncommon but the practice was continued. Two black men, one "a Spanish Mulatto, by name Antonio," were sold by several inhabitants of Boston in 1672 to Virginians for a specified term of seven years labor. Others were manumitted either by legislative decree, by wills and testaments, or by deed. "I sett my negro free," Thomas Whitehead provided in his will of about 1660, " ... he shall be his own man from any person or persons whatsoever." Property was also willed:

> I give my negro man named John all my wearing clothes, my shirts and hatts & shoes and stockings and all that I used to weare. I give unto my negro named John Two cows One called gentle and the other a black heifer & I give him house & ground to plant upon as much as he shall tend himselfe & peaceably to enjoy it his life time without trouble.

In ensuing litigation over the will, it was ruled that the document in effect made John a free man and that he was entitled to the property bequeathed.[21]

The manumitting of blacks continued well into the century and after. But eventually restrictions were placed upon even this practice. In a 1691 law it was noted that "great inconvenience may happen to this country by setting of negroes and mulattoes free by their either entertaining negro slaves or receiving stolen goods or being grown old bringing a charge upon the country (see Document 25).

Within the free black class there were those who had white servants, owned slaves, and possessed varying amounts of property. The contradictory nature of this practice, which continued during the narrowing of status from the 1640s, was dealt with in 1670 when both Negroes and Indians were barred from obtaining labor from certain sources. The question involved was whether Indians or Negroes, having been manumitted or otherwise holding free status could purchase "christian servants," meaning whites. It was ruled that members of either group, "though baptized" and free, could not purchase "christians." However, the assembly did *not* prevent Indians or Negroes "from buying any of their owne nation." In effect, the members of the assembly identified the separateness of white, black, and red groups, a fact of considerable import to the enslavement process, and made certain that whites would not serve or belong to Indians or Africans (*Alternative 4:* see Document 22).

Free blacks, as well as slaves, had other restrictions placed upon them. They were prevented from practicing with the militia and from owning or operating firearms. By 1680, fear of hostile blacks was considerable in the colony. The assembly took note of the frequent meetings of slaves "under the pretence of feasts and buriall" and judged them to be of "dangerous consequence" for the future. In an act designed to render blacks as powerless as possible, the assembly enumerated a considerable number of limitations and punishments upon "any negroe or other slave." The ordinance made it unlawful to carry or be armed with "any club, staffe, gunn, sword or any other weapon of defence or offence." Moreover, physical acts by slaves against whites were prohibited: "if any negroe or other slave shall presume to lift up his hand in opposition against any christian," the offending party was to receive thirty lashes "on his bare back well laid on (see Document 23).

While the presence of free blacks in the latter decades of the seventeenth century in Virginia and elsewhere was evidence of a degree of fluidity within the social structure, in reality the numerous restrictions erected against them demonstrated a deep-rooted hostility and the precariousness of their situation. That they were able to escape enslavement was a reflection of the social ambiguity relative to the question of African status that had characterized colonial society in the early half of the century. Their existence was regarded as an anomaly, a freakish turn of events, and their lives were dogged by many barriers directed at preventing the purchase of property, ownership of dogs, possession of certain drugs and intoxicants, to give some examples. Their inability to serve in the militia and own arms rendered them even more powerless.

Nor was the example of their lives enough to offset or prevent the reduction of other blacks into a state of permanent bondage and eventually into chattel. Ironically, both slavery and freedom were created simultaneously; though they were the antithesis of each other, they developed from common roots. The numerous rulings and laws of the first half of the century did not appear to be affecting the legalization of slavery for the Africans; rather, "they seem more often to be describing and giving legal sanction to practices already in existence."[22] In mid-century, however, it became obvious that distinct separate qualities were being assigned to blacks and whites. By 1670, laws equated blacks with slaves and whites with servants. White became synonymous with freedom, black with its opposite. The one represented dignity, the other degradation.

Laws in the 1670s and 1680s codified these status distinctions. If the rulings removing baptism as a condition of freedom, granting Indians freedom after a specified term of service, and permitting blacks and Indians the right to own only members of their own "nation," as well as the vital wording of other laws listing blacks as slaves, were not clear enough, the enactment of 1682 was harshly explicit. As "an act to repeal a former law [1670] making Indians and others free," it went furthest in detailing who would be deemed a slave. All servants, including "negroes, moores, mollatoes and otheres born of and in heathenish, idollatrous, pagan and mahometan parentage"—though converted to Christianity—"shall be adjudged, deemed and taken to be slaves to all intents and purposes, any law, usage or custome to the contrary notwithstanding." So too were Indians who had been sold by other tribes or to the English to be regarded as slaves. Gone was the distinction of 1670 differentiating between servants who had come by land or sea. Masters were counselled to convert their slaves to the faith, such acceptance no longer having any influence on releasing blacks from bondage. Thus the act recognized a body of nonwhite, Christian workers who were to serve in a permanent state of labor (*Alternative 1:* see Document 24).

Laws in other colonies reflected the developments taking place in Virginia, which indicated a universality of response on the part of the English towards the two nonwhite cultures. In one form or another, legislation was adopted which consigned the African to a slave status or pointed in that direction: Massachusetts in 1641, Connecticut in 1650, Maryland in 1663, New York and New Jersey in 1664, and South Carolina in 1682. Of these, the Maryland law of 1664 was quite specific in the way it established slavery and provided for its perpetuity. The General Assembly ordered that

> all Negroes and other slaves to be hereafter imported into the Province shall serve Durante Vita [for life]. And all Children born of any Negro or other slave shall be Slaves as their fathers were for the term of their lives . . .

To separate the races, the law also contained an antimiscegenation provision. "Freeborn English women" were prohibited from intermarrying with Negro slaves; they were not to be "forgetful of their free Condition" nor that such act was "to the disgrace of our Nation." Women who did become involved in these "Shamefull Matches" were to suffer the loss of considerable freedom for they were to "serve the master of such slaves dureing the life of her husband." The children of such unions were also to be "slaves as their fathers." What of the children of interracial marriages? They were required to serve the masters of their parents until reaching thirty years of age.[23]

Seventeen years later, the Maryland assembly replaced the 1664 law with a more inclusive one. The new ordinance continued the proviso which placed Negroes and other slaves imported or to be imported into slavery "durante vita" but closed what they regarded as loopholes in the earlier act. Masters who enticed their white servant women to intermarry with "Negroes & Slaves" for the illicit purpose of gaining their labor were to lose title to the service of their servants and the women and their children were to be given their freedom. Ten thousand pounds of tobacco was listed as punishment for any master who permitted, and ministers who performed, such marriages between the races.

The laws of Maryland and Virginia of the 1660s through the 1680s, in complementing each other, mark the development of a circular racial equation which remained unbroken until the Civil War *(Alternative 4:* see Document 25). By these ordinances and rulings, the term "servant" meant a limited term of service, "slave" meant permanent bondage; white became synonymous with freedom, black with enslavement. Only servants could be whites, only slaves could be black. By the early part of the eighteenth century, the unabated and uncontested process of enslavement led to the further legalization of the black slave as chattel property.

Yet, despite these decisions and laws, a number of free blacks lived within the colony. These were persons who had been manumitted through wills or some other legal device, or who were born of free black mothers, of a white servant or free woman, of free black parents, or of free black and Indian parentage. The largest percentage were manumitted persons; these were protected in the 1670 act which included "negroes manumitted and otherwise free."

But those blacks who had managed to escape from the entrapment of permanent servitude, though in a better position to maintain control and distance, were nevertheless excluded from social equality and constantly discriminated against. They were in physical danger; laws narrowly circumscribed their social existence. In 1691, for instance, a law prescribed that English "or other white man or woman being free shall intermarry with a negroe, mulatto, or Indian man or woman bond or free, shall within three months after such marriage be banished and removed from this dominion forever ... (see Document 25). Other privileges were denied to the free blacks, such as the right to bear arms, to serve as a witness in court trials, and the right to vote. Though there were a very small number of propertied blacks in the colony, the majority of the blacks were forced into a position of difficulty and degradation.

## Notes

1. Alden T. Vaughan, "Blacks in Virginia: A Note on the First Decade," *William and Mary Quarterly*, 3rd ser., vol. 39 (July, 1972), pp. 469-70.
2. William H. Hening, ed., *Statutes at Large* ... (1823; reprint ed., Charlottesville: University Press of Virginia, 1969), vol. 1, p. 146.
3. Ibid., p. 552.

4. Ibid., p. 226.

5. Helen T. Catterall, *Judicial Cases Concerning American Slavery and the Negro* (New York: Octagon Books, 1968), p. 77.

6. Ibid., p. 30; General Court Records, *Virginia Magazine of History*, vol. 15, no. 11, p. 236.

7. Paul C. Palmer, "Servant into Slave: The Evolution of the Legal Status of the Negro Laborer in Colonial Virginia, "*South Atlantic Quarterly*, vol. 65 (Summer, 1966), pp. 357-58.

8. Hening, ed., *Statutes at Large*, vol. 1, p. 396.

9. Vaughan, "Blacks in Virginia," p. 478.

10. Hening, ed., *Statutes at Large*, vol. 1, p. 360.

11. Warren M. Billings, "The Cases of Fernando and Elizabeth Key: A Note on the Status of Blacks in Seventeenth-Century Virginia," *William and Mary Quarterly*, 3rd ser., vol. 30 (July, 1973), p. 469.

12. Ibid., p. 468.

13. Ibid., p. 470.

14. Winthrop D. Jordan, "Modern Tensions and the Origins of American Slavery," *Journal of Southern History*, vol. 27 (February, 1962), pp. 25-26; Carl N. Degler, *Out of Our Past* (New York: Harper & Row, 1959), pp. 33-34; John H. Russell, *The Free Negro in Virginia, 1619-1865* (Baltimore: Johns Hopkins University Press, 1913), pp. 36-37.

15. Russell, *The Free Negro in Virginia*, p. 34.

16. Susie M. Ames, "County Court Records of Accomack-Northampton Virginia 1632-1640" (American Historical Association, 1954), pp. xxix, xliii, 35.

17. Hening, *Statutes at Large*, vol. 2, p. 170.

18. Ibid., p. 260.

19. Ibid., pp. 270, 277, 267, 282.

20. Ibid., p. 515, Berkeley's emphasis.

21. Russell, *The Free Negro in Virginia*, pp. 39, 49-59.

22. Palmer, "Servant into Slave," p. 370.

23. Archives of Maryland, vol. 1 (1664), pp. 533-34, and vol. 2 (1671), p. 272.

# Epilogue ═══════

## ═══════════The Gestalt

**". . . may not be above one English."**

The decision to make one person free and the other a slave was not of a single moment but of many interactions joined together to form a pattern. The rulings leading up to the establishment of slavery as the condition for Africans and their descendants was the consequence of a process, a working out of problems which appeared at various times. Many of these problems caught people unawares. All along the way to the ultimate conclusion, options existed. As numbers grew and contacts increased, difficulties arose which the colonists felt required legal and institutional resolution. In decisions and rulings over a forty-year period, the English constantly narrowed the areas of interracial relations and thus widened the gap between themselves and Africans and Indians. As they focused upon who they were and projected about who they wanted to become, the colonists also scrutinized the role of the African, those representatives of diverse tribes whose experiences, values, and customs were totally alien to themselves but whose lives were inextricably entwined with their own. Uncertain in the beginning, but not without images and emotions regarding the African, the colonists eventually created a separate social space, a class whose visible features made possible an everlasting social distance.

Only rarely, at least in law, did those who directed the colony—the governors, assemblymen, magistrates, men of old and newly established wealth—make efforts to alter or reverse the situation or widen the social alternatives for blacks. Free blacks were brought or bought into the system, lived and worked with free white persons, but they were the exceptions. And once the institution was embedded into the social fabric, little attention was given to reduce even the grossest aspects of the system. The class space which came to separate the races at the end of the century reflected the social space which existed at the point of contact. Distanced by historical time and culture, the English and African conflicted in subtle ways and communicated on awkward terms. In a strange way the onus was upon the Africans for they had to accommodate to the superior host. Unlike the Indian, who could retain a structured culture and live apart from the English, the Africans were forced to become participants in the community, to become, in essence, like the English. On every level, the African had to learn English ways, habits, customs, attitudes, and the nuances of expression. As victims, they were in the unenviable position of having to assess and mirror their guardians.

It is difficult to tell how well they were able to adapt to English culture. Perhaps they were able to adopt English ways in such a finely tuned manner that the English were thoroughly frightened for their own identities. More likely, however, the English were either put off or amused by the African accents of English words, their attempts to mimic habits, customs, and ways. That blacks were brought and bought into the community, managed and owned property, sired children and intermarried, prayed as baptized Christians, and worked along with whites is clear. That all of these activities were not well received is equally obvious. For shortly after their arrival, rights were diminished and barriers raised. The elite groups used the means at their disposal gradually to force the African into permanent bondage and to ensure separate racial identities. *(Alternatives 3 and 4)*. Not all Englishmen and women were responsive to these actions. Many conceived the role of blacks not as slave, but in a more traditional manner, as a participating member of the community. *(Alternatives 1 and 2)*.

But anxiety about the Africans was considerable. Court decisions reveal concern about religious, sexual, financial, and military matters, all crucial issues to the colony. In an overwhelming number of instances, the legal findings were against the black. Discrimination was a clear pattern of behavior in these affairs. Equally instructive is the partial or complete absence of the black man or woman in other vital areas. In education statutes and census tracts, the Negro was ignored and pertinent information was unlisted. When compared to the treatment of white servants and Indians, many of these omissions appear to be deliberate.

English anxiety about blacks focused on living and interacting with them in daily situations. Consciously or not, the English seem to have been asking certain crucial questions about the psychological and physical nature of Africans relative to themselves: Can this black person become like me? Can "negroes" function like our men and women? Can they be trusted to be like us? Will the children of African and English develop like us or them? What will living and mixing with "negroes" do to us? What the patterns of naming, education statutes, and legal decisions point to is the English concern as to whether the African could become English and conversely, whether permitting the Africans to intermingle with them would lead to an undermining of the community.

The answer to these questions was relatively quick in coming. Over the decades the unaltered direction was towards denial. And once the process of denial was begun, the direction was towards total rejection. With no countervailing institutions or groups to block, ameliorate, or reverse the forces, the blacks suffered the experience of the vulnerable. The psychology of the situation operated against them. With only sporadic efforts being made to educate them, the African was forced to exist on the periphery of society. The African could not remain *within* the community without first becoming similar to the English, and they could not *become* acculturated until actual steps were taken to educate them. It was a vicious, unending circle which trapped the African and directed the colonist towards the conclusion of enslavement.

It would appear, then, that in an environment of precarious existence, Englishmen carefully distinguished between the civilized and the uncivilized; that in an effort to retain an acutely developed sense of *folk*, they separated those influences which threatened to undermine the future of the community. For in the denial of education for the African, the future was thus protected. The colonists were in a position not only to protect the present against radical social and cultural changes but also to enable the culture to be transmitted, intact and improved, from one generation to the next. The laws equating the black as slave—meaning uncivilizable—heightened an already intensely tuned sense of superiority in the English. The refusal to include the Negro in the education statutes was symbolic of the answer to the question posed by the English: can the Negro become like us?

Even educated blacks could fare little better than their uneducated-counterparts. Governor Francis Nicholson, who once proposed the establishment of a free school in Maryland, expressed this sentiment in a letter to the Board of Trade in 1698. "Both in Virginy and here," he observed, " . . . the major part of the Negroes speak English: and most people have some of them as their domestick servants: and the better sort may have 6 or 7 in those circumstances: and may be not above one English."[1] The meaning went in several directions for in Maryland as well as in Virginia by this time the blacks were well on their way to be adjudicated as chattel property. No 'Negro' could therefore be above one English. The fact that the majority of Negroes could speak English was no longer important. In no way would they ever be able to become English.

## Notes

1. Helen T. Catterall, *Judicial Cases Concerning American Slavery and the Negro* (New York: Octagon Books, 1968), vol. 1, p. 54, n. 7.

# Part two

## Documents of the Decision

# 1

# Savage

*Document†*
SA'VAGE. adj.
1. Wild; uncultivated.
   These godlike virtues wherefore do'st thou hide,
   Affecting private life, or more obscure
   In *savage* wilderness?

   *Milton.*

   Cornels, and *savage* berries of the wood,
   And roots and herbs, have been my meagre food.

   *Dryden.*

2. Untamed; cruel.
   Chain me to some sleepy mountain's top,
   Where roaring bears and *savage* lions roam.

   *Shakespeare.*

   Tyrants no more their *savage* nature kept,
   And foes to virtue wonder'd how they wept.

   *Pope.*

3. Uncivilized; barbarous; untaught.
   Hence with your little ones:
   To fright you thus, methinks, I am too *savage;*
   To do worse to you, were fell cruelty.

   *Shakespeare, Macbeth.*

   Thus people lived altogether a *savage* life, 'till Saturn, arriving on those
   coasts, devised laws to govern them by.

   *Raleigh.*

   The *savage* clamour drown'd
   Both harp and voice.

   *Milton.*

   A herd of wild beasts on the mountains, or a *savage* drove of men in
   caves, might be so disordered; but never a peculiar people.

   *Spratt's Sermons.*

†From: Samuel Johnson, *A Dictionary of the English Language,* (London, 1805), vol. 1.

# 2

# William Crashaw's Sermon, 1610

*Document†*

... Hereby we shall honour ourselves and strengthen ourselves by propagating our owne religion: hereby we shall mightily advance the honourable name of the English nation, the honor whereof we ought every one to seek: hereby we shall mightily inrich our nation, strengthen our navie, fortifie our kingdome, and be lesse beholding to other nations for their commodities: and to conclude, hereby we shall rectifie and reforme many disorders which in this mightie and populous state are scarce posibly to be reformed without evacuation: and consequentlie when we have atchieved all these ends, we shall eternize our owne names to all ensuing posteritie as being the first beginners of one of the bravest and most excellent exploits that was attempted since the Primitive times of the Church .... Therefore let all nations see, to their amazement, the divels to their terror, the Angels to their joy, and especially Our God to his glorie, and the honor of his truth, that the English Christians will not undertake a publike action which they will not prosecute to perfection. Let us then beleeve no tales, regard no slanders (raised or spred by Papists or Epicures) feare no shadowes, care for no oppositions, respect no losses that may befall, nor bee daunted with any discouragements whatsoever; but goe forward to assist this noble action with countenance and counsell, with men and money, and with continuall supplies, till wee have made our plantation and Colonie able to subsiste of itselfe, and till there be a Church of God established in Virginea, even there where Satans throne is. Thus shall we honour our God, our religion, our Nation, and leave that honour on our names, which shall make them flourish till the worlds end, and (which is all in all) lay up that comfort for our soules which shall stand by us at our deaths, & speake for us to the Great Judge at the last and great day.

And to you (right honourable and beloved) who ingage your lives, and therefore are deepliest interested in this businesse, who make the greatest ventures, and beare the greatest burdens; who leave your ease and pleasures at home, and commit yourselves to the Seas and winds for the good of this enterprise; you that desire to advance the Gospell of Jesus Christ, though it be with the hazard of your lives, goe forward in the name of the God of heaven and earth, the God that keepeth covenant and mercie for thousands; goe on with the blessing of God, Gods Angels and Gods Church; cast away feare, and let nothing daunt your spirits, remembering whom you goe unto, even to the

†From: Alexander Brown, ed., *The Genesis of the United States* (New York: Houghton Mifflin Co., 1890), vol. 1, pp. 367-71.

Englishmen your brethren, who have broke the ice before you, and suffered that which with God's blessing you never shall; remembring what you goe to doe, even to display the banner of Christ Jesus, to fight with the divell and the old dragon, having Michael and his Angels on your side: to eternize your owne names both heere at home & amongst the Virgineans (whose Apostles you are) and to make yourselves most happy men whether you live or die: if you live, by effecting so glorious a worke; if you die, by dying as Martyrs or Confessors of God's religion: and remembring lastly whom you leave behinde you, even us your brethen, of whom many would goe with you that yet may not, many will follow you in convenient time, and who will now goe with you in our hearts and praiers, and who will second you with New & fresh supplies, & who are resolved (by the grace of that God in whose name they have undertaken it) never to relinquish this action; but though all the wealth already put in were lost, will againe & againe renue and continue their supplies, untill the Lord give the hoped harvest of our endevors.

And thou most noble Lord, who God hath stirred up to neglect the pleasure of England, and with Abraham to goe from thy country, and forsake thy kindred and thy fathers house, to goe to a Land which God will shew thee, give me leave to speake the truth: Thy Ancestor many hundred yeeres ago gained great honour to thy house; but by this action thou augmentist it. He tooke a king prisoner in the field in his owne Land: but by the godly managing of this businesse, thou shalt take the divell prisoner in open field, and in his own kingdome: Nay the Gospell which thou carriest with thee shall binde him in chaines, and his Angels in stronger fetters then iron, and execute upon them the judgement that is written: Yea it shall lead Captivity Captive, and redeeme the soules of men from bondage. And thus thy glory and honour of thy house is more at the last then at the first.

Goe on therefore, and prosper with this thy honor, which indeed is greater then every eie discernes, even such as the present ages shortly will enjoy, and the future admire: Goe forward in the strength of the Lord thy God, and make mention of his righteousnesse only. Looke not at the gaine, the wealth, the honour, the advancement of thy house that may follow and fall upon thee: but looke at those higher and better ends that concerne the Kingdome of God. Remember thou art a Generall of English men, nay a Generall of Christian men; therefore principally looke to religion. You goe to commend it to the heathen, then practice it yourselves: make the name of Christ honourable, not hatefull unto them. Suffer no Papists; let them not nestle there; nay let the name of the Pope or Poperie be never heard of in Virginea. Take heed of Atheists the Divels Champions: and if thou discover any, make them exemplarie. And (if I may be so bold as to advise) make Atheisme and other blasphemie Capitall, and let that bee the first law made in Virginia. Suffer no Brownists, nor factious Separatists: let them keepe their conventicles elsewhere: let them goe and convert some other Heathen, and let us see if they can constitute such Churches really, the Idaes whereof they have fancied in their branes: and when they have given us any such example, we may then have some cause to follow them. Till then we will take our paterne from their betters. Especially suffer no sinfull, no leaud, no licentious men, none that live not under the obedience of good lawes: and let your lawes be strict, especially against swearing and other prophanenesse. And though vaine swearing by Gods name be the common and crying sinne of England, and no morrall, but a veniall sinne in Popish doctrine, yet know that it is a sinne under which the earth mournes: and your land will flourish if this be repressed. Let the Sabboth be wholly and holily observed, and publike praiers daily frequented, idlenesse eschewed, and mutinies carefully prevented. Be well advised in making lawes: but being made, let them be obeyed, and let none stand for scarre-crowes; for that is the way to make all at last to be contemned. This course taken, and you shall see those who were to blame at home, will proove praise-worthy in Virginea. And you will teach us in England to know (who almost have forgotten it) what an excellent thing execution of lawes is in a common-wealth. But if you should aime at nothing but your private ends, and neglect religion and God's service, looke for no blessing, nay looke for a curse, though not on the whole action, yet on our attempt; and never thinke that we shall have the honour to effect it. Yet thinke not that our sinne shall hinder the purpose of God: for when this sinfull generation is consumed, God will stirre up our children after us, who will learne by our example to follow it in more holy manner, and so bring it to that perfection which we for our sinnes and prophanenesse could not doe. But you (right honourable) have otherwise learned Christ, and (we hope) will other-wise practise him, and will declare by your managing of this action the power of that true religion you have learned in England. Thus shall heaven and earth blesse you, and for this heroicall adventure of thy person and state in such a godly cause, the God of heaven will make thy name to bee remembred thorowout all generations: and thousands of people shall honour thy memorie, and give thankes to God for thee while the world endureth.

And thou Virginea, whom though mine eies see not, my heart shall love; how hath God honoured thee! Thou hast thy name from the worthiest Queene that ever the world had: thou hast thy matter from the greatest King on earth: and thou shall now have thy forme from one of the most glorious Nations under the Sunne, and under the conduct of a Generall of as great and ancient Nobility as ever was ingaged in action of this nature. But this is but a little portion of thy honour: for thy God is coming towards thee, and in the meane time sends to thee, and salutes thee with the best blessing heaven hath, even his blessed Gospell. Looke up therefore, and lift up thy head, for thy redemption draweth nie: and he that was the God of Israel, and is still the God of England, will shortly I doubt not bring it to passe, that men shall say, Blessed be the Lord God of Virginea; and let all Christian people say. Amen.

And this salutation doth my soule send thee, O Virginea, even this poor New-yeeres gift, who though I be not worthy to be thine Apostle, yet doe vow and devote myselfe to be in England thy faithfull factor and solicitor, and most desirous to do thee any service in the Lord Jesus Christ our Saviour and then: whom we beseech for his standard amonst you, and that you may once crie for yourselves as we do now for you, Even so come Lord Jesus.

# 3

# Civility

*Document†*

CIVI′LITY. n.s.

1. Freedom from barbarity; the state of being civilised.

The English were at first as stout and warlike a people as ever the Irish; and yet are now brought unto that *civility*, that no nation in the world excelleth them in all goodly conversation, and all the studies of knowledge and humanity.

*Spenser's State of Ireland.*

Divers great monarchies have risen from barbarism to *civility*, and fallen again to ruin.

*Davies on Ireland.*

Wheresoe'er her conquering eagles fled,
Arts, learning, and *civility* were spread.

*Denham's Poems.*

2. Politeness; complaisance; elegance of behaviour.

Art thou thus bolden'd, man, by thy distress;
Or else a rude despiser of good manners,
That in *civility* thou seem'st so empty?

Shakespeare, *As you like it.*

He, by his great *civility* and affability, wrought very much upon the people.

*Clarendon, b. viii.*

I should be kept from a publication; did not what your *civility* calls a request, your greatness, command.

*South.*

We, in point of *civility*, yield to others in our own houses.

*Swift.*

Rule of decency; practise of politeness.
Love taught him shame; and shame, with love at strife,
Soon taught the sweet *civilities* of life.

*Dryden Cym. and Iphig.*

To CI′VILIZE. v.a.

To reclaim from savageness and brutality; to instruct in the arts of regular life.

We send the graces and the muses forth,
To *civilize* and to instruct the North.

*Waller.*

Musaeus first, then Orpheus *civilize*
Mankind, and gave the world their deities.

*Denham.*

†From: Samuel Johnson, *Dictionary*, vol. 1.

Amongst those who are counted the *civilized* part of mankind, this original law of nature still takes place.

Locke.

Osiris, or the Bacchus of the antients, is reported to have *civilized* the Indians, and reigned amongst them fifty-two years.

Arbuthnot on Coins.

CI′VILIZER. n.s.

He that reclaims others from a wild and savage life; he that teaches the rules and customs of civility.

The *civilizers!*—the disturbers, fay;—
The robbers, the corrupters of mankind!
Proud vagabonds!

Philips's Briton.

# 4

# Of the Naturall Inhabitants of Virginia

*Document†*

The land is not populous, for the men be fewe; their far greater number is of women and children. Within 60 miles of James Towne there are about some 5000 people, but of able men fit for their warres scarse 1500. To nourish so many together they have yet no means, because they make so smal a benefit of their land, be it never so fertill. 6 or 700 have beene the most [that] hath beene seene together, when they gathered themselves to have surprised Captaine Smyth at Pamaunke, having but 15 to withstand the worst of their furie. As small as the proportion of ground that hath yet beene discovered, is in comparison of that yet unknowne. The people differ very much in stature, especially in language, as before is expressed. Some being very great as the Sesquesahamocks, others very little as the Wighcocomocoes: but generally tall and straight, of a comely proportion, and of a colour browne, when they are of any age, but they are borne white. Their haire is generally black; but few have any beards. The men weare halfe their heads shaven, the other halfe long. For Barbers they use their women, who with 2 shels will grate away the haire, of any fashion they please. The women are cut in many fashions agreeable to their yeares, but ever some part remaineth long. They are very strong, of an able body and full of agilitie, able to endure to lie in the woods under a tree by the fire, in the worst of winter, or in the weedes and grasse, in Ambuscado in the Sommer. They are inconstant in everie thing, but what feare constraineth them to keepe. Craftie, timerous, quicke of apprehension and very ingenuous. Some are of disposition fearefull, some bold, most cautelous, all Savage. Generally covetous of copper, beads, and such like trash. They are soone moved to anger, and so malitious, that they seldome forget an injury: they seldome steale one from another, least their conjurors should reveale it, and so they be pursued and punished. That they are thus feared is certaine, but that any can reveale their offences by conjuration I am doubtfull. Their women are carefull not to bee suspected of dishonesty without the leave of their husbands. . . .

†From: John Smith, *A Map of Virginia, With a Description of the Country, the Commodities, People and Religion* (Oxford: Joseph Barnes, 1612).

# 5

# A Brief Description of the People, May 21- June 21, 1607

*Document†*

There is a king in this land called great Pawatah, under whose dominions are at least 20$^{ty}$ severall kingdomes, yet each king potent as a prince in his owne territory. these have their Subiectes at so quick Comaund, as a beck bringes obedience, even to the resticucion of stolne goodes which by their naturall inclinac[i]on they are loth to leave. They goe all naked save their privityes, yet in coole weather they weare deare skinns, with the hayre on loose: some have leather stockings up to their twists, & sandalls on their feet, their hayre is black generally, which they weare long on the left side, tyed up on a knott, about which knott the kinges and best among them have a kind of Coronett of deares hayre coloured redd, some have chaines of long linckt copper about their neckes, and some chaines of pearle, the common sort stick long fethers in this knott, I found not a grey eye among them all. their skynn is tawny not so borne, but with dying and paynting them selves, in which they delight greatly. The women are like the men, onely this difference; their hayre groweth long al over their heades save clipt somewhat sort afore, these do all the labour and the men hunt and goe at their plesure. They live comonly by the water side in litle cottages made of canes and reedes, covered with the barke of trees; they dwell as I guesse by families of kindred & allyance some 40$^{tie}$ or 50$^{tie}$ in a Hatto or small village; which townes are not past a myle or half a myle asunder in most places. They live upon sodden wheat beanes & peaze for the most part, also they kill deare take fish in their weares, & kill fowle aboundance, they eate often and that liberally; they are proper lusty streight men very strong runn exceeding swiftly, their feight is alway in the wood with bow & arrowes, & a short wodden sword, the celerity they use in skirmish is admirable. the king directes the batle & is alwayes in front. Their manner of entertainment is upon mattes on the ground under some tree, where they sitt themselves alone in the midest of the matt, & two mattes on each side, on which they[r] people sitt, then right against him (making a square forme) satt we alwayes. when they came to their matt they

†From: Philip Barbour, ed., *The Jamestown Voyages Under the First Charter, 1606-1609* (Cambridge: Hakluyt Society, 1969), vol. 1, pp. 102-104.

have an usher goes before them, & the rest as he sittes downe give a long showt. The people steale any thing comes neare them, yea are so practized in this act that lookeing in our face they would with their foot betwene their toes convey a chizell knife, percer or any indifferent light thing: which having once conveyed they hold it an iniury to take the same from them; They are naturally given to trechery, howbeit we could not finde it in our travell up the river, but rather a most kind and loving people. They sacrifice Tobacco to the Sunn fayre picture or a harmefull thing, as a sword or peece also; they strincle some into the water in the morning before they wash. they have many wives, to whome as neare as I could perceive they keep constant. the great king Pawatah had most wives: These they abide not to be toucht before their face. the great diseaze reignes in the men generally, full fraught with noodes botches and pulpable apparances in their forheades, we found above a hundred. The wemem are very cleanly in making their bread and prepareing meat. I found they account after death to goe into an other world pointing eastward to the Element, and when they saw us at prayer they observed us with great silence and respect especially those to whome I had imparted the meaning of our reverence. To conclude they are a very witty and ingenious people, apt both to understand and speake our language, so that I hope in god as he hath miraculously preserved us hither from all dangers both of sea and land & their fury so he will make us authors of his holy will in converting them to our true Christian faith by his own inspireing grace and knowledge of his deity.

# 6

# Instructions to George Yeardley, 1618

*Document†*

... And Whereas by a special Grant and licence from his Majesty a general Contribution over this Realm hath been made for the building and planting of a college for the training up of the Children of those Infidels in true Religion moral virtue and Civility and for other godly uses We do therefore according to a former Grant and order hereby ratifie confirm and ordain that a convenient place be chosen and set out for the planting of a University at the said Henrico in time to come and that in the mean time preparation be there made for the building of the said College for the Children of the Infidels according to such Instructions as we shall deliver And we will and ordain that ten thousand acres partly of the Lands they impaled and partly of other Land within the territory of the said Henrico be alotted and set out for the endowing of the said University and College with convenient possessions. ...

†From: S.M. Kingsbury, ed., *Records of the Virginia Company of London* (Washington, D.C.: Library of Congress, 1906), vol. 3, p. 102.

# 7

# Report of the Treasurer on Funds for Henrico College, 1619

*Document†*

It was also by m$^r$ T͠rer propounded to the Co$^{rt}$ as a thing most worthy to be taken into consideracͦon both for the glory of God, and hono$^r$ of the Company, that forasmuch as the King in his most gracious favo$^r$ hath graunted his L͠res to the severall Bishops of this Kingdome for the collecting of monies to erect and build a Colledge in Virginia for the trayning and bringing up of Infidells children to the true knowledge of God & understanding of righteousnes. And considering what publique notice may be taken in foreslowing to sett forward the accon, especially of all those w$^{ch}$ hath contributed to the same, that therefore to begin that pious worke, there is allready towards it—1500$^{li}$,—or thereabouts, whereof remayning in cash 800$^{li}$, the rest is to be answered out of the Stock of the Generall Company for so much w$^{ch}$ they borrowed, besides the likelihood of more to come in; ffor m$^r$ Teasuro$^r$ having some conference w$^{th}$ the Bishop of Lichfield, he hath not heard of any Colleccͦon that hath beene for that busines in his Diocese; but promiseth when he hath a warr$^t$ thereunto he will w$^{th}$ all dilligence further the enterprize; Whereupon he conceaved it the fittest; that as yet they should not build the Colledge, but rather forbeare a while; and begin first with the meanes they have to provide and settle an Annuall revennue, and out of that to begin the ereccͦon of the said Colledge: And for the performance hereof also moved, that a certaine peece of Land be Laid out at Henrico being the place formerly resolved of w$^{ch}$ should be called the Colledge Land, and for the planting of the same send presently ffifty good persons to be seated thereon and to occupy the same according to order, and to have halfe the benefitt of their Labo$^r$ and the other halfe to goe in setting forward the worke, and for mayntenance of the Tuto$^{rs}$ & Schollers. He therefore propounded that a Shipp might be provided against the begining of August, to carry those ffifty men w$^{th}$ their provisions, as also to send ffiftie persons more to the Comon Land w$^{ch}$ may raise a Stock for the paying of dueties there and defraying the Companies charge here, and to send provision of victuals w$^{th}$ them for a yeare: And for the defraying the charge hereof did

†From: Kingsbury, ed., *Records of the Virginia Company*, vol. 1, pp. 220-21.

also propound the meanes; first for the Colledge there was mony in Cash, and besides it may save the Ioint stock the sending out a Shipp this yeare, w^ch for 4^d a pound they will bring from thence all their Tobacco w^ch may arise to ffive hundreth pounde besides mony that may come in otherwise to [8] helpe to beare the charge of the voyage; W^ch Proposicõn was well liked but the time and season not allowed of all; and by some obiected, that the Generall Plantacõn should receave much mony if more men were sent over soe sodaynly before those that are allready gone have procured wherew^thall to subsist; as also being a matter of greate consequence it did more propperly belong to the deciding of a Quarter Co^rt: but the former reasons being answered; and being further alleaged if it were till then prolonged the time would be past for their provisions of beefe, beere, and meate. Whereupon after Long arguing and disputing thereof it was agreed to be putt to the question; W^ch being propounded whether a shipp should be sett out to carry men for these two good uses and be sett out at the publique charge—(viz^t) w^th 50 Passengers for the Colledge Land, and 50 for the Comon Land, it was by generall consent, and erecõn of hande allowed and confirmed.

# 8

# John Smith's Thoughts on the Massacre

*Document†*

Thus have you heard the particulars of this massacre, which in those respects some say will be good for the Plantation, because now we have just cause to destroy them by all meanes possible: but I thinke it had beene much better it had never happened, for they have given us an hundred times as just occasions long agoe to subject them, ... Moreover, where before we were troubled in cleering the ground of great Timber, which was to them of small use: now we may take their owne plaine fields and Habitations, which are the pleasantest places in the Countrey. Besides, the Deere, Turkies, and other Beasts and Fowles will exceedingly increase if we beat the Salvages out of the Countrey: for at all times of the yeare they never spare Male nor Female, old nor young, egges nor birds, fat nor leane, in season or out of season; with them all is one. The like they did in our Swine and Goats, for they have used to kill eight in tenne more then we, or else the wood would most plentifully abound with victuall; besides it is more easie to civilize them by conquest then faire meanes; for the one may be made at once, but their civilizing will require a long time and much industry. The manner how to suppresse them is so often related and approved, I omit it here: And you have twenty examples of the Spaniards how they got the West-Indies, and forced the treacherous and rebellious Infidels to doe all manner of drudgery worke and slavery for them, themselves living like Souldiers upon the fruits of their labours. This will make us more circumspect, and be an example to posteritie: (But I say, this might as well have beene put in practise sixteene yeares agoe as now).

Thus upon this Anvill shall wee now beat our selves an Armour of proofe hereafter to defend us against such incursions, and ever hereafter make us more circumspect: but to helpe to repaire this losse, besides his Majesties bounty in Armes he gave the Company out of the Tower, and divers other Honorable persons have renewed their adventures, we must not omit the Honorable Citie of London, to whose endlesse praise wee may speake it, are now setting forward one hundred persons: and divers others at their owne costs are a repairing; and all good men doe thinke never the worse of the businesse for all these disasters.

What growing state was thereever in the world which had not the like? ...

†From: John Smith, *The Generall Historie of Virginia, New-England, and the Summer Isles, With the Names of the Adventurers, Planters, and Governors From Their First Beginning. An: 1584 to This Present 1624* (London: Printed by I.D. and I.H. for Michael Sparken, 1624).

# 9

## Laws of Virginia, 1623-1624

*Document†*

23. That every dwelling house shall be pallizaded in for defence against the Indians.
24. That no man go or send abroad without a sufficient partie will armed.
25. That men go not to worke in the ground without their arms (and a centinell upon them.)
26. That the inhabitants go not aboard ships or upon any other occasions in such numbers, as thereby to weaken and endanger the plantations.
27. That the commander of every plantation take care that there be sufficient of powder and amunition within the plantation under his command and their pieces fixt and their arms compleate.
28. That there be dew watch kept by night.
29. That no commander of any plantation do either himselfe or suffer others to spend powder unnecessarily in drinking or entertainments, &c.
30. That such persons of quality as shall be founde delinquent in their duties being not fitt to undegoe corporal punishment may notwithstanding be imprisoned at the discretione of the commander & for greater offences to be subject to a ffine inflicted by the monthlie court, so that it exceed not the value aforesaid.
31. That every man that hath not contributed to the finding a man at the castell shall pay for himself and servants five pounds of tobacco a head, towards the discharge of such as had their servants there.
32. That the beginning of July next the inhabitants of every corporation shall fall upon their adjoyning salvages as we did the last yeare, those that shall be hurte upon service to be cured at the publique charge; in case any be lamed to be maintained by the country according to his person and quality.
33. That for defraying of such publique debts our troubles have brought upon us. There shall be levied 10 pounds of tobacco upon every male head above sixteen years of adge now living (not including such as arrived since the beginning of July last.)
34. That no person within this colony upon the rumur of supposed change and alteration, presume to be disobedient to the present

†From: William W. Hening, ed., *Statutes at Large: Being a Collection of all the Laws of Virginia from the First Session of the Legislature in the Year 1619* (1823; reprint ed., Charlottesville: University Press of Virginia, 1969), vol. 1, pp. 126-28.

government, nor servants to their private officers, masters or overseers at their uttermost perills.

ACT VIII.

It is also ordered, That the warr begun uppon the Indians bee effectually followed, and that noe peace bee concluded with them. And likewise that all marches which shall hereafter bee ordered and appoynted against them, be prosequted and followed with all dilligence.

# 10

# A Declaration of the State of the Colonie and Affairs in Virginia

*Document†*
... With a Relation to the barbarous Massacre in the time of peace and League, treacherously executed upon the *English by the native Infidels*, 22 March last (1622).

Thus have you seene the particulars of this massacre, out of Letters from thence written, wherein treachery and cruelty have done their worst to us, or rather to themselves; for whose understanding is so shallow, as not to perceive that this must needs bee for the good of the Plantation after, and the losse of this blood to make the body more healthfull, as by these reasons may be manifest.

First, Because betraying of innocency never rests unpunished. ...

Secondly, Because our hands which before were tied with gentlenesse and faire usage, are now set at liberty by the treacherous violence of the Savages, not untying the Knot, but cutting it: So that we, who hitherto have had possession of no more ground then their waste, and our purchase at a valuable consideration to their owne contentment, gained; may now by right of Warre, and law of Nations, invade the Country, and destroy them who sought to destroy us: whereby wee shall enjoy their cultivated places, turning the laborious Mattocke into the victorious Sword (wherein there is more both ease, benefit, and glory) and possessing the fruits of others labours. Now their cleared grounds in all their villages (which are situate in the fruitfullest places of the land) shall be inhabited by us, whereas heretofore the grubbing of woods was the greatest labour.

Thirdly, Because those commodities which the Indians enjoyed as much or rather more than we, shall now also be entirely possessed by us. The Deere and other beasts will be in safety, and infinitly increase, which heretofore not onely in the generall huntings of the King (whereat foure or five hundred Deere were usually slaine) but by each particular Indian were destroied at all times of the yeare, without any difference of Male, Damme, or Young. The

†From: S.M. Kingsbury, ed., *Records of the Virginia Company*, vol. 3, pp. 556-58.

like may be said of our owne Swine and Goats, whereof they have used to kill eight in tenne more than the English have done. There will be also a great increase of wild Turkies, and other waighty Fowle, for the Indians never put difference of destroying the Hen, but kill them whether in season or not, whether in breeding time, or sitting on their egges, or having new hatched, it is all one to them: whereby, as also by the orderly using of their fishing Weares, no knowne Country in the world will so plentifully abound in victuall.

Fourthly, Because the way of conquering them is much more easie then of civilizing them by faire meanes, for they are a rude, barbarous, and naked people, scattered in small companies, which are helps to Victorie, but hinderances to Civilities: Besides that, a conquest may be of many, and at once; but civility is in particular, and slow, the effect of long time, and great industry. Moreover, victorie of them may bee gained many waies; by force, by surprize, by famine in burning their Corne, by destroying and burning their Boats, Canoes, and Houses, by breaking their fishing Weares, by assailing them in their huntings, whereby they get the greatest part of their sustenance in Winter, by pursuing and chasing them with our horses, and blood-Hounds to draw after them, and Mastives to teare them, which take this naked, tanned, deformed, Savages, for no other then wild beasts, and are so fierce and fell upon them, that they feare them worse then their old Devill which they worship, supposing them to be a new and worse kinde of Devils then their owne. By these and sundry other wayes, as by driving them (when they flye) upon their enemies, who are round about them, and by animating and abetting their enemies against them, may their ruine or subjection be soone effected. . . .

# 11

# Indian Education, Connecticut, 1654

*Document†*

Whereas, notwithstanding former provision made for the conveyance of the knowledge of God to the natives amongst us, little hath hitherto been attended through want of an able interpreter, this Court being earnestly desirous to promote and further what lies in them a work of that nature, wherein the glory of God and the everlasting welfare of those poor, lost, naked sons of Adam is so deeply concerned, do order that Thomas Mynor, of Pequot, shall be wrote unto from this Court and desired that he would forthwith send his son, John Mynor, to Hartford, where this Court will provide for his maintenance and schooling, to the end he may be for the present assistant to such elder, elders or others, as this Court shall appoint to interpret the things of God to them as he shall be directed, and in the meantime to fit himself to be instrumental that way as God shall fit and incline him thereunto for the future.

†From: Elsie W. Clews, *Educational Legislation and Administration of the Colonial Governments* (New York: Macmillan Co., 1899), p. 111.

# 12

# "They are not Deficient in Natural Understanding"

*Document†*

Philadelphia May 9th, 1753

Sir

I received your Favour of the 29th. August last and thank you for the kind and judicious remarks you have made on my little Piece. Whatever further occurs to you on the same subject, you will much oblige me in communicating it. . . .

We had here some years since a Transylvanian Tartar, who had travelled much in the East, and came hither merely to see the West, intending to go home thro' the spanish West Indies, China &c. He asked me one day what I thought might be the Reason that so many and such numerous nations, as the Tartars in Europe and Asia, the Indians in America, and the Negroes in Africa, continued a wandring careless Life, and refused to live in Cities, and to cultivate the arts they saw practiced by the civilized part of Mankind. While I was considering what answer to make him; I'll tell you, says he in his broken English, God make man for Paradise, he make him for to live lazy; man make God angry, God turn him out of Paradise, and bid him work; man no love work; he want to go to Paradise again, he want to live lazy; so all mankind love lazy. Howe'er this may be it seems certain, that the hope of becoming at some time of Life free from the necessity of care and Labour, together with fear of penury, are the mainsprings of most peoples industry.

To those indeed who have been educated in elegant plenty, even the provision made for the poor may appear misery, but to those who have scarce ever been better provided for, such provision may seem quite good and sufficient, these latter have then nothing to fear worse than their present Conditions, and scarce hope for any thing better than a Parish maintainance; so that there is only the difficulty of getting that maintainance allowed while they are able to work, or a little shame they suppose attending it, that can induce them to work at all, and what they do will only be from hand to mouth.

The proneness of human Nature to a life of ease, of freedom from care and labour appears strongly in the little success that has hitherto attended every attempt to civilize our American Indians, in their present way of living,

†From: Leonard W. Larabee and Whitfield J. Bell, Jr., eds., *The Papers of Benjamin Franklin* (New Haven, Conn.: Yale University Press, 1961), pp. 479-83.

almost all their Wants are supplied by the spontaneous Productions of Nature, with the addition of very little labour, if hunting and fishing may indeed be called labour when Game is so plenty, they visit us frequently, and see the advantages that Arts, Sciences, and compact Society procure us, they are not deficient in natural understanding and yet they have never shewn any Inclination to change their manner of life for ours, or to learn any of our Arts; When an Indian Child has been brought up among us, taught our language and habituated to our Customs, yet if he goes to see his relations and make one Indian Ramble with them, there is no perswading him ever to return, and that this is not natural [to them] merely as Indians, but as men, is plain from this, that when white persons of either sex have been taken prisoners young by the Indians, and lived a while among them, tho' ransomed by their Friends, and treated with all imaginable tenderness to prevail with them to stay among the English, yet in a Short time they become disgusted with our manner of life, and the care and pains that are necessary to support it, and take the first good Opportunity of escaping again into the Woods, from whence there is no reclaiming them. One instance I remember to have heard, where the person was brought home to possess a good Estate; but finding some care necessary to keep it together, he relinquished it to a younger Brother, reserving to himself nothing but a gun and a match-Coat, with which he took his way again to the Wilderness.

Though they have few but natural wants and those easily supplied. But with us are infinite Artificial wants, no less craving than those of Nature, and much more difficult to satisfy; so that I am apt to imagine that close Societies subsisting by Labour and Arts, arose first not from choice, but from necessity: When numbers being driven by war from their hunting grounds and prevented by seas or by other nations were crowded together into some narrow Territories, which without labour would not afford them Food. However as matters [now] stand with us, care and industry seem absolutely necessary to our well being; they should therefore have every Encouragement we can invent, and not one Motive to diligence be subtracted, and the support of the Poor should not be by maintaining them in Idleness; But by employing them in some kind of labour suited to their Abilities of body &c. as I am informed of late begins to be the practice in many parts of England, where work houses are erected for that purpose. If these were general I should think the Poor would be more careful and work voluntarily and lay up something for themselves against a rainy day, rather than run the risque of being obliged to work at the pleasure of others for a bare subsistence and that too under confinement. The little value Indians set on what we prize so highly under the name of Learning appears from a pleasant passage that happened some years since at a Treaty between one of our Colonies and the Six Nations; when every thing had been settled to the Satisfaction of both sides, and nothing remained but a mutual exchange of civilities, the English Commissioners told the Indians, they had in their Country a College for the instruction of Youth who were there taught various languages, Arts, and Sciences; that there was a particular foundation in favour of the Indians to defray the expense of the

Education of any of their sons who should desire to take the Benefit of it. And now if the Indians would accept of the Offer, the English would take half a dozen of their brightest lads and bring them up in the Best manner; The Indians after consulting on the proposal replied that it was remembered some of their Youths had formerly been educated in that College, but it had been observed that for a long time after they returned to their Friends, they were absolutely good for nothing being neither acquainted with the true methods of killing deer, catching Beaver or surprizing an enemy. The Proposition however, they looked on as a mark of the kindness and good will of the English to the Indian Nations which merited a grateful return; and therefore if the English Gentlemen would send a dozen or two of their Children to Onondago the great Council would take care of their Education, bring them up in really what was the best manner and make men out of them. . . .

# 13

# Laws of Virginia, December, 1656

*Document†*

ACT II

Concerning orphans estates, *Be it from henceforth enacted*, That all will and testaments be firme and inviolable, but in case the executors or overseers refuse to execute their trust, then the estates disposed of by will to be liable to such rules as are laid down for the management of estates of persons intestate.

That noe accounts be allowed on orphans estates, but they to be educated upon the interest of the estate, if it will beare it, according to the proportion of their estate, But if the estate be so meane and inconsiderable that it will not reach to a free education then that orphan be bound to some manuall trade till one and twenty yeares of age, except some ffriends or relations be willing to keep them with the increase of that small estate, without diminution of the principall, which whether greate or small allways to returne to the orphans at the yeares appointed by law.

That all cattell, horses and sheep be returned in kind by the guardians, according to age and number, whereat he received them, as all household stuff, lumber and the like to be prized in money, And by the guardians to be paid in the country comodity (whatsoever it shall be) to the orphans as it is then currant in the country and in the perticular place where the orphan's estate is managed.

That the court take able and sufficient security for orphans estates, and enquire yearly of the security, & if the court sees cause, to have it changed or called in and placed as the court shall think best, The said court also to enquire whether orphans be kept and maintained and educated according as their estates will beare, And if they find any notorious defect to remove the orphans to other guardians, As also for those that are bound apprentices to change their master if he use them rigourously or neglect to teach them his trade.

That such orphans as are not bound apprentices shall after seaventeen yeares of age have the produce of their owne labours and industry and to dispose of as they list, besides the maintenance from their guardians, Allwaies provided that nothing be infringed.

That no more be allowed to guardians for collecting of debts due to the estate then what is allowed usually by merchants to their ffactors or

†From: Hening, ed., *Statutes at Large*, vol. 1, pp. 416-17.

attorneys, or rather that so much in the hundred be appointed as shall seem reasonable to the courts.

That thirty pounds of tobacco per day and no more be allowed to each apprizer for the apprizement of all estates if they will take it.

That there be a regulation of excessive ffuneral charges by the commissioners where nothing is mentioned concerning them in the decedents will.

# 14

# Laws of Virginia, September, 1632

*Document†*

ACT VII

*IT is thought fitt,* That uppon every Sonday the mynisters shall halfe an hower or more before eveninge prayer examine, catechise, and instruct the youth and ignorant persons of his parish in the ten commandments, the articles of the beliefe and the Lords prayer. And shall diligentlie heere, instruct and teach them the catichisme, sett forth in the booke of comon prayer, and all ffathers, mothers, maysters, and mistrisses shall cause theire children, servants, and apprentizes which have not learned the catichisme to come to the church at the tyme appoynted obedientlie to heere and to be ordered by the mynister until they have learned the same. And yf any of the said ffathers, mothers, maysters, or mistrisses, children, servants, or apprentizes shall neglect theire duties as the one sort in not causinge them to come, and the other in refusinge to learne as aforesayd, they shall be censured by the corts in those places holden.

†From: Hening, ed., *Statutes at Large*, vol. 1, pp. 181-82.

# 15

# Duke's Law of the State of New York, 1664

*Document†*

Whereas it is highly necessary and of great consequence that the youth, from their childhood, is well instructed in reading, writing and arithmetic, and principally in the principles and fundaments of the Christian religion, in conformity to the lesson of that wise King Solomon, 'Learn the youth the first principles, and as he grows old, he shall then not deviate from it;' so that in time such men may arise from it, who may be able to serve their country in Church or in State; which being seriously considered by the Director General and Council in New Netherland, as the number of children by God's merciful blessing has considerably increased, they have deemed necessary, so that such an useful and to our (us) God agreeable concern may be more effectually promoted, to recommend the present schoolmaster, and to command him, so as it is done by this, that they (Pietersen, the Principal, and Von Hoboocken, of the branch school on the Bouwery) on Wednesday, before the beginning of the sermon, with the children entrusted to their care, shall appear in the church to examine, after the close of the sermon, each of them his own scholars, in the presence of the reverend ministers and elders who may there be present, what they, in the course of the week, do remember of the Christian commands and catechism, and what progress they have made; after which the children shall be allowed a decent recreation.

Done in Amsterdam, New Netherland, this 17th March, 1664, by the Director General and Council.—Dunshee, 30.

†From: Ecclesiastical Records of the State of New York (Albany, 1901), vol. 1, p. 542.

# 16

# "Of Children and Their Education"

*Document†*

God, that made all things good, and blessed them, imparted expressly this blessing first to his creatures, capable thereof, that they should increase and multiply in their kind. More especially, God created our first parents, male and female, and blessed them, saying, "Be fruitful, and multiply, and fill the earth." This order then set, he hath preserved to this day, and mankind by it. By this, parents when they are dead, live in their children as parts of them, and imps [Grafts] taken from their stock, and in special manner, one with them. ... And let us remember, that as brutes bring forth in their kind, and all parents their children; so we, being in the Lord's covenant of grace, bring forth, as by nature ours, so by the supernatural covenant and grace, his children also; and that he trusts us with the bringing them up for him, and in his nurture and instruction; which is a great matter, and wherein we must deal faithfully with him; that so under his blessing, we may fit them for his heavenly inheritance, provided for them with us. It is a during fruit of God's gracious covenant, when good parents by their godly care have gracious children; and that by which our faith is much confirmed.

Children, in their first days, have the greater benefit of good mothers, not only because they suck their milk, but in a sort, their manners also, by being continually with them, and receiving their first impressions from them. But afterwards, when they come to riper years, good fathers are more behoveful for their forming in virtue and good manners, by their greater wisdom and authority: and ofttimes also, by correcting the fruits of their mothers's indulgence, by their severity. [Aristotle.]

They are a blessing great, but dangerous. They come into the world at first with danger, both in respect of themselves, as passing sometimes, from the womb to the grave; sometimes, being born deformed in body; sometimes, incapable of understanding: as also in regard of the mother, the first day of their being in the world, being often her last in it. After their coming into the world through so many dangers, they come even into a world of dangers. In their infancy, how soon is the tender bud nipped, or bruised by sickness or otherwise! In their venturesome days, into how many needless dangers do they throw themselves, in which many perish, besides those into which God brings them, and that all their life long! Above all other, how great and many are their spiritual dangers, both for nourishing and increasing the corruption

†From: John Robinson, *The Works of John Robinson, Pastor of the Pilgrim Fathers* (London: John Snow, 1851), pp. 242-49.

which they bring into the world with them; and for diverting them from all goodness, which God's grace, and men's endeavour might work in them! These dangers and difficulties, howsoever they make not God's blessings in giving children to be no blessings, or deserving to be lightly esteemed; yet should they moderate our desire of them, and grief for their want: that none should say either to God or one to another, as Rachel did to Jacob, "Give me children, or else I die," Gen. xxx. 1: specially if we weigh withal, that though the Lord give us divers towardly, and good; yet one or two proving lewd and wicked will break our tender hearts, more than all the rest will comfort us: like as in the natural body there is more grief by the aching of some one part, though but a tooth, than comfort and ease in the good and sound state of all the rest. If children considered aright of the careful thoughts, sorrows and fears, and sore pains withal of their parents, they would think they owed them more honour, service and obedience, than, for the most part, they do. We seldom consider and prize worthily the cares and pains of parents, till we become parents ourselves, and learn them by experience.

Many bodily diseases are hereditary; and so are many spiritual, in a sort; and that both by natural inclination, and moral imitation much more: that, as the Lord saith of Israel, "Thou art thy mother's daughter," Ezek. xvi. 45, so may it be said of many, that they are their fathers' and mothers' sons and daughters in evil. Yet, if it so come to pass, that God vouchsafe grace to the child of a wicked father, and that he see the sins which he hath done, he commonly hates them more vehemently, than if they had been in a stranger; and good reason, considering how they have been his dearest parent's ruin. Yea further, even where grace is wanting, the child, ofttimes, by observing and sometimes by feeling also the evil of his father's sin, is driven, though not from his evil way into a good way, yet into the contrary evil. Thus a covetous father often makes a prodigal son; so doth a prodigal a covetous. The son of the covetous taking knowledge how odious his father's covetousness is to all; and therewith persuading himself, and being persuaded by others about him, that there is enough, and more than enough for him, takes occasion as prodigally to pour out, as his father hath miserly hoarded up: as on the contrary, the son of the prodigal both seeing, and feeling the hurt of his parent's lavishness, is thereby provoked to lay the harder about him, for the repairing of his father's ruins.

Love rather descends, than ascends; as streams of water do; and no marvel, if men love where they live, as parents do in children, and not they in them. Hence also is it, that grandfathers are more affectionate towards their children's children, than to their immediates, as seeing themselves further propagated in them, and by their means proceeding on to a further degree of eternity, which all desire naturally, if not in themselves, yet in their posterity. And hence it is, that children brought up with their grandfathers, or grandmothers, seldom do well, but are usually corrupted by their too great indulgence.

It is much controverted, whether it be better, in the general, to bring up children under the severity of discipline, and the rod, or no. And the wisdom of the flesh out of love to its own, alleges many reasons to the contrary. But say men what they will, or can, the wisdom of God is best; and that saith, that "foolishness is bound up in the heart of a child, which the rod of correction must drive out:" and that "he, who spares his rod, hurts his son," Prov. xxii. 15; xiii. 24; not in the affection of person, but effect of thing. And surely there is in all children, though not alike, a stubbornness, and stoutness of mind arising from natural pride, which must, in the first place, be broken and beaten down; that so the foundation of their education being laid in humility and tractableness, other virtues may, in their time, be built thereon. This fruit of natural corruption and root of actual rebellion both against God and man must be destroyed, and no manner of way nourished, except we will plant a nursery of contempt of all good persons and things, and of obstinacy therein. It is commendable in a horse, that he be stout and stomachful, being never to be left to his own government, but always to have his rider on his back, and the bit in his mouth. But who would have his child like his horse in his brutishness? Indeed such as are of great stomach, being thoroughly broken, and informed, become very serviceable, [Erasmus] for great designs: else, of horses they become asses, or worse: as Themistocles; master told him, when he was a child, that either he would bring some great good, or some great hurt to the commonwealth. [Plutarch] Neither is there need to fear, lest by this breaking, the children of great men should prove basespirited and abject, and so unapt to great employments: for being Adam's sons, whose desire was to have been like unto God, and having those advantages for masterfulness and high thoughts, which great men's children want not, unto whom great affairs are appropriated usually, they will not easily be found unfurnished of stomach and stoutness of mind more than enough; wherein a little is dangerous, specially for making them unmeet for Christ's yoke, and to learn of him, who was lowly, and meek. Matt. xi. 29.

For the beating, and keeping down of this stubbornness parents must provide carefully for two things: first that children's wills and wilfulness be restrained and repressed, and that, in time; lest sooner than they imagine, the tender sprigs grow to that stiffness, that they will rather break than bow. Children should not know, if it could be kept from them, that they have a will in their own, but in their parents' keeping: neither should these words be heard from them, save by way of consent, "I will" or "I will not." And, if will be suffered at first to sway in them in small and lawful things, they will hardly after be restrained in great and ill matters, which their partial conceit, and inexperienced youth, with the lusts thereof and desire of liberty, shall deem small and lawful, as the former. And though good education, specially the grace of God, may afterwards purge out much other evil and weaken this also: yet will such unbroken youth most commonly draw after it great disquietness in crosses, when they fall; and in the whole course of life, a kind of unwieldiness, inflexibility and obstinacy, prejudicial to the parties themselves and uncomfortable, at least, to such as converse with them. The second help is an inuring of them from the first, to such a meanness in all things, as may rather pluck them down, than lift them up: as by plain, and homely diet, and apparel; sending them to school betimes; and bestowing them afterwards, as they are fit, in some course of life, in which they may be exercised diligently, and the same rather under than above their estate: by not abetting them one against another, nor against any, specially before their faces, without great cause: nor by making them men and women, before they become good boys and girls. How oft have I observed, that parents, who have neither failed in diligent instructing of their children, nor in giving them good example, nor in correcting them duly, have only by straining too high this way, either endangered, or utterly overthrown their posterity! hereby lifting them up in their vain hearts, and teaching them to despise both mean things and persons; and themselves also, many times, amongst others: thereby drowning them, Icarus like, in a sea of mischief and misery, by their flying too high a pitch. And this must be the more minded, because there is in men an inbred desire, and that inordinate usually, to hoist up their children, as high, as may be: so as they half think they do them wrong, if they set them not higher, or as high, as least, as themselves, almost whether God will or no. Yes what place affords not some such, as make themselves their children's slaves, not caring how basely they themselves grovel in the earth, so they may set them on their tiptoes.

But first of all for children's competent education, specially for their disposing in some particular course, on which all are to settle at last, though some liberty of stepping this way, or that be given them for a while; as a man, though for his pleasure he see many places, yet seeks his abode in some one in the end, [Plutarch] there is required in their parents a thorough discerning and right judgment of their disposition; which is as difficult, as necessary. The difficulty ariseth from the partiality of parents towards their own: for that as the crow thinks her own bird fairest, so do they commonly their children towardly, and better than they are, or than any other indifferent judge both. This partiality in many is so gross, as they not only deem small good things in them, great, and great evils, small; but often account the same things well becoming them and commendable, which in others they would censure as indecent, and it may be, enormous. This pernicious error ariseth from self-love. For, as in nature, the object cannot be seen, which is either too near the eye, or too far from it; so neither can the disposition of that child be rightly discerned, which lieth too near his father's heart. And yet is the knowledge of this, so necessary, that we build not either upon a vain, or uncertain foundation, with great hazard of loss, both of labour, and expense, in sorting our child to his particular calling and course of life; as all without it, is but a very rash adventure. For as none are fit for every course, nor hardly any for many, in any great degree, so every one is fit for one or other: to which if his ability, and disposition be applied, with any convenient diligence on his part and helps by others; he may easily come to a mediocrity therein, if not to some rareness. Hence was it, that fathers in some places, used to lead their children to the shops of all kind of artificers, to try how they could both handle their tools, and like their works; that so they might bestow them accordingly. Some wise men also have wished, that there might be established, by public authority, a course for the due trial, and choice of wits for several sciences. And surely, where there goes not before a natural aptness and moral disposition also for some calling; there will follow nothing but loss: loss of time, loss of labour, loss of charges, and all; as when the seed is cast into the barren ground. And as the midwife how skilful soever in her art, cannot make the woman to be delivered, that was not first with child; so neither can the best masters make their scholars, or servants, to bring forth sciences, unless they have an aptness thereunto first conceived in their brains. [Plato]. . . .

# 17

# A Proposition for Encouraging the Christian Education of Indian, Negro, and Mulatto Children

*Document†*

It being a duty of Christianity very much neglected by masters and mistresses of this country (America) to endeavour the good instruction and education of their heathen slaves in the Christian faith,—the said duty being likewise earnestly recommended by his Majesty's instructions,—for the facilitating thereof among the young slaves that are born among us; it is, therefore, humbly proposed that every Indian, negro, or mulatto child that shall be baptized and afterward brought to church and publicly catechized by the minister in church, and shall, before the fourteenth year of his or her age, give a distinct account of the Creed, the Lord's Prayer, and Ten Commandments, and whose master or mistress shall receive a certificate from the minister that he or she hath so done, such Indian, negro, or mulatto child shall be exempted from paying all levies till the age of eighteen years.

†From: Sadie Bell, *The Church, the State and Education in Virginia* (New York: Arno Press, 1969), p. 30.

# 18

# Contract for Negroes, 1642

*Document†*

Leonard Calvert Esq. etc. acknowledged that he hath conveyed and sold unto John Skinner mariner, all those his 3 Mannors of St. Michael, St. Gabriel, and Trinity Mannor, with all the tenements and hereditaments in or upon them or any of them, and all his right title and interest in and to the premises or any part thereof, to have and to hold the same to the said John Skinner his heires and assignes for ever. And that he hath further covenanted to finish the dwelling house at Pinie neck, with a stack of brick chimneyes (conteining 2 chimneys) neare about the middle of the house now standing and to make the partition by the said chimneyes, and doores and windowes, and to underpin the frame of it wth stone or brick. In consideration wherof the said John Skinner covenanted and bargained to deliver unto the said Leonard Calvert, fourteene negro men-slaves, and three women slaves, of betweene 16 and 26 yeare old able and sound in body and limbs, at some time before the first of march come twelve-month, at St. Maries, if he bring so many within the Capes, by himselfe or any assignes betweene this and the said first of march, or afterward within the said yeare, to be delivered as aforesaid to him the said Leonard Calvert or his assignes in the case aforesaid. And in case he shall not so doe, then he willeth and granteth that foure and twenty thousand weight of tobacco, be leavied upon any the lands goods or chattells of him the said John Skinner, to the use of him the said Leonard Calvert and his assignes.

†From: Elizabeth Donnan, *Documents Illustrative of the History of the Slave Trade in America* (New York: Octagon Books, 1969), vol. 4, p. 8.

# 19

# Narrative of Olaudah Equiano

*Document†*

We practised circumcision like the Jews, and made offerings and feasts on that occasion in the same manner as they did. Like them also our children were named from some event, some circumstance, or fancied foreboding, at the time of their birth. I was named Olaudah, which in our language, signifies vicissitude, or fortune also; one favoured, and having a loud voice, and well spoken. I remember we never polluted the name of the object of our adoration; on the contrary, it was always mentioned with the greatest reverence; and we were totally unacquainted with swearing, and all those terms of abuse and reproach which find their way so readily and copiously into the language of more civilized people. The only expressions of that kind I remember were "May you rot, or may you swell, or may a beast take you."

†From: Olaudah Equiano, *The Interesting Narrative of Olaudah Equiano, or Gustavus Vasa, The African* (London, 1789), p. 79.

# 20

# Laws of Virginia, March 1661-1662

*Document†*

ACT CII, Run-aways.

WHEREAS there are diverse loytering runaways in this country who very often absent themselves from their masters service and sometimes in a long time cannot be found, that losse of the time and the charge in the seeking them often exceeding the value of their labor: *Bee it therefore enacted* that all runaways that shall absent themselves from their said masters service, shalbe lyable to make satisfaction by service after the times by custome or indenture is expired (vizt.) double their times of service soe neglected, and if the time of their running away was in the crop or the charge of recovering them extraordinary the court shall lymitt a longer time of service proportionable to the damage the master shall make appeare he hath susteyned, and because the adjudging the time they should serve is often referred untill the time by indenture is expired, when the proofe of what is due is very uncertaine, *it is enacted* that the master of any runaway that intends to take the benefitt of this act, shall as soone as he hath recovered him carry him to the next commissioner and there declare and prove the time of his absence, and the charge he hath bin at in his recovery, which commissioner thereupon shall grant his certificate, and the court on that certificate passe judgment for the time he shall serve for his absence; and in case any English servant shall run away in company of any negroes who are incapable of making satisfaction by addition of a time, *it is enacted* that the English soe running away in the company with them shall at the time of service to their owne masters expired, serve the masters of the said negroes for their absence soe long as they should have done by this act if they had not beene slaves, every christian in company with them shall by proportion among them, either pay fower thousand five hundred pounds of tobacco and caske or fower yeares service for every negroe soe lost or dead.

†From: Hening, ed., *Statutes at Large*, vol. 2, pp. 116-17.

# 21

# Laws of Virginia, October, 1669

*Document†*

ACT I, An act about the casuall killing of slaves.

WHEREAS the only law in force for the punishment of refractory servants (a) resisting their master, mistris or overseer cannot be inflicted upon negroes, nor the obstinacy of many of them by other then violent meanes supprest, *Be it enacted and declared by this grand assembly,* if any slave resist his master (or other by his masters order correcting him) and by the extremity of the correction should chance to die, that his death shall not be accompted ffelony, but the master (or that other person appointed by the master to punish him) be acquit from molestation, since it cannot be presumed that prepensed malice (which alone makes murther ffelony) should induce any man to destroy his owne estate.

†From: Hening, ed., *Statutes at Large,* vol. 2, p. 270.

# 22

# Laws of Virginia, October, 1670

*Document†*

ACT V, Noe Negroes nor Indians to buy christian servants.

WHEREAS it hath beene questioned whither Indians or negroes manumited, or otherwise free, could be capable of purchasing christian servants. *It is enacted* that Noe negroe or Indian though baptised and enjoyed their owne ffeedome shall be capable of any such purchase of christians, but yet not debarred from buying any of their owne nation.

†From: Hening, ed., *Statutes at Large*, vol. 2, pp. 280-81.

# 23

# Laws of Virginia, June, 1680

*Document†*

ACT X, An act for preventing Negroes Insurrections.

WHEREAS the frequent meeting of considerable numbers of negroe slaves under pretence of feasts and burialls is judged of dangerous consequence; for prevention whereof for the future, *Bee it enacted by the kings most excellent majestie by and with the consent of the generall assembly, and it is hereby enacted by the authority aforesaid,* that from and after the publication of this law, it shall not be lawfull for any negroe or other slave to carry or arme himselfe with any club, staffe, gunn, sword or any other weapon of defence or offence, nor to goe or depart from of his masters ground without a certificate from his master, mistris or overseer, and such permission not to be granted but upon perticuler and necessary occasions; and every negroe or slave soe offending not haveing a certificate as aforesaid shalbe sent to the next constable, who is hereby enjoyned and required to give the said negroe twenty lashes on his bare back well layd on, and soe sent home to his said master, mistris or overseer. *And it is further enacted by the authority aforesaid* that if any negroe or other slave shall presume to lift up his hand in opposition against any christian, shall for every such offence, upon due proofe made thereof by the oath of the party before a magistrate, have and receive thirty lashes on his bare back well laid on. *And it is hereby further enacted by the authority aforesaid* that if any negroe or other slave shall absent himself from his masters service and lye hid and lurking in obscure places, comitting injuries to the inhabitants, and shall resist any person or persons that shalby and lawfull authority be imployed to apprehend and take the said negroe, that then in case of such resistance, it shalbe lawfull for such person or persons to kill the said negro or slave soe lying out and resisting, and that this law be once every six months published at the respective country courts and parish churches within this colony.

†From: Hening, ed., *Statutes at Large*, vol. 2, pp. 481-82.

# 24

# Laws of Virginia, November, 1682

*Document†*

ACT I, An act to repeale a former law making Indians and others ffree.

WHEREAS by the 12 act of assembly held att James Citty the 3d day of October, Anno Domini 1670, entituled an act declareing who shall be slaves, *it is enacted* that all servants not being christians, being imported into this country by shipping shall be slaves, but what shall come by land shall serve if boyes and girls untill thirty yeares of age, if men or women, twelve yeares and noe longer; and for as much as many negroes, moores, mollatoes and others borne of and in heathenish, idollatrous, pagan and mahometan parentage and country have heretofore, and hereafter may be purchased, procured, or otherwise obteigned as slaves of, from or out of such their heathenish country by some well disposed christian, who after such their obteining and purchaseing such negroe, moor, or molatto as their slave out of a pious zeale, have wrought the conversion of such slave to the christian faith, which by the laws of this country doth not manumitt them or make them free, and afterwards such their conversion, it hath and may often happen that such master or owner of such slave being by some reason inforced to bring or send such slave into this country to sell or dispose of for his necessity or advantage, he the said master or owner of such servant which notwithstanding his conversion is really his slave, or his factor or agent must be constrained either to carry back or export againe the said slave to some other place where they may sell him for a slave, or else depart from their just right and tytle to such slave and sell him here for noe longer time then the English or other christians are to serve, to the great losse and damage of such master or owner, and to the great discouragement of bringing in such slaves for the future, and to noe advantage at all to the planter or buyer; and whereas alsoe those Indians that are taken in warre or otherwise by our neighbouring Indians, confederates or tributaries to his majestie, and this his plantation of Virginea are slaves to the said neighbouring Indians that soe take them, and by them are likewise sold to his majesties subjects here as slaves, *Bee it therefore enacted by the governour councell and burgesses of this general assembly, and it is enacted by the authority aforesaid*, that all the said recited act of the third of October 1670 be, and is hereby repealed and made utterly voyd to all intents and purposes whatsoever. *And be it further enacted by the authority aforesaid* that all servants except Turkes and Moores, whilest in amity with

†From: Hening, ed., *Statutes at Large*, vol. 2, pp. 490-92.

his majesty which from and after publication of this act shall be brought or imported into this country, either by sea or land, whether Negroes, Moors, Mollattoes or Indians, who and whose parentage and native country are not christian at the time of their first purchase of such servant by some christian, although afterwards, and before such their importation and bringing into this country, they shall be converted to the christian faith; and all Indians which shall hereafter be sold by our neighbouring Indians, or any other trafiqueing with us as for slaves are hereby adjudged, deemed and taken, and shall be adjudged, deemed and taken to be slaves to all intents and purposes, any law, usage or custome to the contrary notwithstanding.

# 25

# Laws of Virginia, April, 1691

*Document†*

ACT XVI, An act for suppressing outlying Slaves.

WHEREAS many times negroes, mulattoes, and other slaves unlawfully absent themselves from their masters and mistresses service, and lie hid and lurk in obscure places killing hoggs and committing other injuries to the inhabitants of this dominion, for remedy whereof for the future, *Be it enacted by their majesties lieutenant governour, councell and burgesses of this present generall assembly, and the authoritie thereof, and it is hereby enacted,* that in all such cases upon intelligence of any such negroes, mulattoes, or other slaves lying out, two of their majesties justices of the peace of that county, whereof one to be of the quorum, where such negroes, mulattoes or other slave shall be, shall be impowered and commanded, and are hereby impowered and commanded to issue out their warrants directed to the sherrife of the same county to apprehend such negroes, mulattoes, and other slaves, which said sherriffe is hereby likewise required upon all such occasions to raise such and soe many forces from time to time as he shall think convenient and necessary for the effectual apprehending such negroes, mulattoes and other slaves, and in case any negroes, mulattoes or other slave or slaves lying out as aforesaid shall resist, runaway, or refuse to deliver and surrender him or themselves to any person or persons that shall be by lawfull authority employed to apprehend and take such negroes, mulattoes or other slaves that in such cases it shall and may be lawfull for such person and persons to kill and distroy such negroes, mulattoes, and other slave or slaves by gunn or any otherwaise whatsoever.

*Provided* that where any negroe or mulattoe slave or slaves shall be killed in pursuance of this act, the owner or owners of such negro or mulatto slave shall be paid for such negro or mulatto slave four thousand pounds of tobacco by the publique. And for prevention of that abominable mixture and spurious issue which hereafter may encrease in this dominion, as well by negroes, mulattoes, and Indians intermarrying with English, or other white women, as by their unlawfull accompanying with one another, *Be it enacted by the authoritie aforesaid, and it is hereby enacted,* that for the time to come, whatsoever English or other white man or woman being free shall intermarry with a negroe, mulatto, or Indian man or woman bond or free shall within three months after such marriage be banished and removed from

†From: Hening, ed., *Statutes at Large,* vol. 3, pp. 86-88.

this dominion forever, and that the justices of each respective countie within this dominion make it their perticular care, that this act be put in effectuall execution. *And be it further enacted by the authoritie aforesaid, and it is hereby enacted*, That if any English woman being free shall have a bastard child by any negro or mulatto, she pay the sume of fifteen pounds sterling, within one moneth after such bastard child shall be born, to the Church wardens of the parish where she shall be delivered of such child, and in default of such payment she shall be taken into the possession of the said Church wardens and disposed of for five yeares, and the said fine of fifteen pounds, or whatever the woman shall be disposed of for, shall be paid, one third part to their majesties for and towards the support of the government and the contingent charges thereof, and one other third part to the use of the parish where the offence is committed, and the other third part to the informer, and that such bastard child be bound out as a servant by the said Church wardens untill he or she shall attaine the age of thirty yeares, and in case such English woman that shall have such bastard child be a servant, she shall be sold by the said church wardens, (after her time is expired that she ouhht by law to serve her master) for five yeares, and the money she shall be sold for divided as is before appointed, and the child to serve as aforesaid.

And forasmuch as great inconveniences may happen to this country by the setting of negroes and mulattoes free, by their either entertaining negro slaves from their masters service, or receiveing stolen goods, or being grown old bringing a charge upon the country; for prevention thereof, *Be it enacted by the authority aforesaid, and it is hereby enacted*, That no negro or mulatto be after the end of this present session of assembly set free by any person or persons whatsoever, unless such person or persons, their heires, executors or administrators pay for the transportation of such negro or negroes out of the countrey within six moneths after such setting them free, upon penalty of paying of tenn pounds sterling to the Church wardens of the parish where such person shall dwell with, which money, or so much thereof as shall be necessary, the said Church wardens are to cause the said negro or mulatto to be transported out of the countrey, and the remainder of the said money to imploy to the use of the poor of the parish.

# Part three

# Bibliographic Essay

# Overview of an Historical Debate

Extending almost three-fourths of a century, the scholarly debate over the origins and institutionalization of slavery is now extensive and complex. In the nineteenth century, slave apologists and pseudo-anthropoligists generally ascribed historical and biological factors as the cause of slavery. The presumption was that the first Africans who disembarked in Virginia and Maryland became slaves partly because of their having been captured, transported, and sold, not unlike the millions of Africans who had been enslaved in the West Indies prior to 1619 or those countless millions throughout history who have been captured in war and used as permanent laborers. American slavery, then, resulted from external forces which were internationally recognizable and historically acceptable. A related argument centered on the alleged innate inferiority of the African. Turning to ancient and contemporary philosophers, from Plato and Aristotle to Sir Thomas More, and utilizing questionable anthropological data, slavery rationalizers simply stated that slave status was natural for the Africans because of their stunted development. George Sawyer, a member of the Louisiana bar, noted in his 1859 apologia, *Southern Institutions, or An Inquiry into the Origins and Early Prevalance of Slavery and the Slave Trade, etc., in Defence of the Southern Institutions* (Philadelphia: J.B. Lippincott, 1859): "Measured by the size, weight, and capacity of the brain, they are inferior to the race of aborigines of America" (p. 185). Sawyer concluded that slavery was the only natural state for the African. "The die is cast; nature has assigned the condition of the Negro race, and fixed the limits of their destiny" (p. 201).

Scholarly justification for believing that Africans had become slaves immediately after disembarking in Virginia was based on some evidence. John Rolfe's bland remark, recorded by John Smith in 1620,—"About the last of August came in a dutch man of warre that sold us twenty Negars"—conveyed a sense of completeness. In "Virginia" a concise essay on the subject, Edgar T. Thompson correctly surmised why many have erroneously interpreted the situation. "Perhaps because John Rolfe used the term 'sold' in his journal, and because Negro slaves later were sold, it has been assumed that complete slavery was introduced in Virginia in 1619." This essay is included in *Race: Individual and Collective Behavior*, eds. Edgar T. Thompson and Everett C. Hughes, (New York: Free Press, 1958), p. 259.

But the problems of role and status are difficult to assess because of the scarcity of data and the apparent indeterminacy of the African's position. Were distinctions made between white indentured servants and black laborers from initial contact or did they evolve over a period of time? What was the nature of relationships between the races in the first decades? How were Africans regarded? What variables should be used to analyze the problem?

Early twentieth-century historians challenged the 'natural state' bias and the notion of instantaneous and "complete slavery." The first major investigation was James C. Ballagh's *A History of Slavery in Virginia* (Baltimore: Johns Hopkins Press, 1902). Ballagh held that the first Africans in the colony were not "slaves in the strict sense of the term" (p. 28). Basing his argument on international considerations, Ballagh stated on page 28 that "as captives, not of warfare, but of privacy, they were under the protection of international law in maintaining their original status, and had they been citizens of a powerful civilized community they might have received it."

Blacks were thus legally "but colony servants" in the early years of their servitude and "a disposition to recognize them as such seems apparent." Ballagh noted that some Negroes received wages, bought their freedom, and that the length of the servitude frequently depended upon conversion to Christianity. "Servitude not only preceded slavery in the logical development of the principle of subjection," Ballagh concluded, "but it was the historic base upon which slavery, by the extension and addition of incidents, was constructed" (pp. 31-32).

Ballagh's thesis was accepted and expanded by John H. Russell in *The Free Negro in Virginia, 1619-1865* (Baltimore: John Hopkins Press, 1913). In examining the nature and development of a body of free blacks in Virginia, Russell took note of the absence of slavery in England and its probable ramifications in the colony:

Since it is the fact that the white population in the colony in 1619 had not been familiar in England with a system of slavery or with a model of a slave code, and since they had developed in Virginia a system of servitude and were fortifying it by law, it is plausible that the Africans became servants in a condition similar to the status of white servants . . . (p. 23).

As evidence, Russell cited the "lists of living and dead in Virginia in 1623 and the "Muster Rolls of the Settlements in Virginia," a census taken in 1624-1625, in which all of the twenty-three Africans in the colony were listed as "servants," the identical class-name given to white persons on the lists. Nor were Africans listed as anything but "servants," "negroes," or "negro servants" in county records dating from 1632 to 1661. Russell presented evidence of blacks who sued for their freedom or who became landowners. Thus, the implication of the Ballagh-Russell thesis was that the development of racist perceptions and behavior derived from the institutionalization of slavery itself.

Despite the careful analyses by Ballagh and Russell, the thesis of outright slavery was continued by several scholars well into the twentieth century. "He was seized in Africa with slavery in mind," wrote Avery Craven in *The Repressible Conflict* (Baton Rouge: Louisiana State University Press, 1939). "He was sold outright in America. A few may have become indentured servants in the American colonies in the early period, but experience soon proved that system too liberal for Negroes raw out of Africa" (p. 41).

Studies which promulgated the proposition that servitude preceded and influenced slavery focused heavily upon the relationship between environmental and economic factors. In the first major Afro-American history, a remarkable two volume work by a black historian which appeared in 1883, George Washington Williams presaged several of the positions on slavery's origins. In his *History of the Negro Race in America, 1619-1880*, 2 vols. (New York: George Putnam and Co., 1883), Williams suggested four factors which inevitably doomed the Negro: "the latitude, the products of the soil, the demand for labor, the custom of the indenture of white servants, were abundant reasons why the Negro should be doomed to bondage for life" (pp. 1, 120). Other historians of the Old South narrowed the causes to land and labor supply. Thomas J. Wertenbaker in *The Old South* (New York: Charles Scribner's Sons, 1942), decried slavery itself, maintaining that "it was this very superabundance of riches which in the end proved the curse of the South. It was the soil . . . which brought on the South the curse of Slavery. With land, rich land in almost ulimited quantities to be had at very low prices, the constant demand was for cheap labor" (p. 5). Since the supply of labor was always low and transportation costs of indentured servants high, the Negro was preferable. R.S. Cotterill in *The Old South* (Glendale, Ca.: Arthur R. Cook, 1939) argued for the uniqueness of the situation. "In Virginia and Maryland the settlers adopted slavery slowly and reluctantly as a thing alien to all his English experience and repulsive to his English ideals . . ." (p. 80). What produced slavery, in Cotterill's view, was the inevitable requirement for labor stability. "Permanency, not skill, was the quality that was most needed in a labor supply for the South, and the only possible solution was slavery." Clement Eaton, in his widely used text, *A History of the Old South* (New York: Macmillan Co., 1949) held that slavery was the result of inexorable forces. In classical economic terms, Eaton contended that "its establishment in the South was the natural outgrowth of economic 'laws', especially Wakefield's law, which laid down the premise that the presence of plentiful and cheap land suitable for agriculture and the lack of labor bred slavery." Eaton added harshly that men seldom will work "for free wages when they can become independent farmers" (p. 45).

Similarly, in his influential works on slavery, *American Negro Slavery* (New York: D. Appleton & Co., 1918) and *Life and Labor in the Old South* (Boston: Little, Brown & Co., 1929), Ulrich B. Phillips viewed the origins of slavery as deriving from the concept of property. Unlike Wertenbaker, however, Phillips attempted to diminish the harshness of slavery, comparing it with alimony. Phillips began his important chapter "The Peculiar Institution" in the latter book by noting that for an individual to be regarded as property "may seem barbaric and outrageous." But, in the twentieth century, he continued, "thousands of divorced husbands are legally required to pay periodic alimony to their ex-wives, and if one seeks escape from the levy upon his earnings, he may be clapped into prison until he gives adequate pledges of compliance" (p. 160). Proceeding to more serious considerations of origins, however, Phillips sided with Ballagh and Russell. Slaves were property and "in a civilized order property needs definition and official recognition ..." (p. 161). Racial factors, though, entered into Phillips's hypothesis. In a later publication, *The Course of the South to Secession* (New York: D. Appleton-Century Co., 1939). Phillips more fully explained the concept of racial awareness and white superiority. "Slavery was instituted not merely to provide control of labor but also as a system of racial adjustment and social order." (p. 152).

In *A History of the South* (New York: Alfred A. Knopf, 1947), Francis Simkins elaborated Phillips's racial conceptions. Negroes were a greater menace to the biological integrity of the white race than the native Indians because they were more dangerous, Simkins asserted. "They adjusted easily to the ways of the white man." Consequently, as soon as the blacks became numerous, "a wall of caste was erected against them" (p. 25). Simkins pinpointed the relationship between the two major forces in southern history. Within the span of a single lifetime, "two of the most dominant institutions of southern society—white supremacy and African slavery—were well established," (p. 24; 1972 edition with Charles P. Roland). Simkins's evidence for English racial attitudes rested upon the colonists' failure to develop sexual contact with Indian women. English men might have turned to the "lure of Indian women" but this was "checkmated by the importation of English women" (p. 24).

An important challenge to the Ballagh-Russell thesis that servitude preceded and shaped slavery was advanced in 1940 by Susie M. Ames in *Studies of the Virginia Eastern Shore* (1940; reissue, New York: Russell and Russell, 1973). Ames contended that there were not enough examples to support the accepted thesis; free blacks could have been slaves who were set free by their masters, or were the offspring of emancipated persons, or even offspring of mulattoes. Ames was extremely doubtful about the possibility of early servant status of Africans. There were instances of Negroes serving for specified terms, she agreed, but in most cases it was very difficult "to tell whether the 'indenture' was a voluntary surrender by the master of further service due him or merely the customary procedure" (p. 104). Ames was backed up by Wesley Frank Craven in his broad study, *The Southern Colonies in the Seventeenth Century, 1607-1689* (Baton Rouge: Louisiana State University Press, 1949), who felt that a "sharp distinction" existed between the African and white servant from the very beginning. Though the black's situation might vary according to the attitudes of the individual master, Craven argued, most of the "peculiar problems of slave discipline were adequately covered by an increasingly elaborate servant code" (pp. 217-19).

Oscar and Mary Handlin, in an article published the following year, countered Ames and Craven and essentially supported the majority thesis. It would be logical, the Handlins stated, to assume with Russell that free blacks had been servants who had completed their terms. In the "The Origins of the Southern Labor System" *William and Mary Quarterly*, 3rd ser. vol. 7 (April, 1950), pp. 199-222, reprinted in Oscar Handlin, *Race and Nationality in American Life* (Boston: Little, Boston, Brown & Co., 1957), the Handlins flatly asserted that, "an examination of the conditions and status of seventeenth-century labor will show that slavery was not there from the start, that it was not simply imitated from elsewhere, and that it was not a response to any unique qualities in the Negro himself" (p. 199). How, then, did slavery come into being? "It emerged from the adjustment to American conditions of traditional European institutions."

The traditional European institutions to which the Handlins refer were the systems of villenage and involuntary bondage and the laws which defined limitations upon human action. In seventeenth-century England, the laws recognized gradations of servility, the lowest position being not one of slave but of relative "unfreedom." In the transference of this labor system to the colonies, these degrees were maintained. The first generation Africans were accepted into society as relatively "unfree" servants and, as such, enjoyed whatever privileges were granted to white indentured servants. "These newcomers, like so many others, were accepted, bought, and held as kind of servants" (p. 203 and n. 13).

If Negroes were incorporated into society with a status approximately equivalent to that of indentured servants, what factors operated to force them into slavery? The Handlins pointed to the adjustment of the colonist as capitalist. Simply stated, the major factor was the desire for a larger labor force to fill the needs of an expanding economy at a time when the migration from England was contracting. To encourage immigration it became necessary to ameliorate the condition of the white indentured servant by shortening the terms of indenture and by ensuring a future as freeperson and landowner. Blacks were omitted from these enactments of expectancy and hope, for there was no one in England or in the colonies to pressure for a lessening of their labor period or to fight for their future. By mid-century, the work term of the Negroes "seems generally lengthier than that of the whites; and thereafter the consciousness dawns that the Blacks will toil for the whole of their lives, not through any particular concern with their status but simply by contrast with those whose years of labor are limited by statute" (p. 211). Inevitably, color became a sign of slave status and just as inevitably slave status connoted a type of chattel property. "The identical steps that made the slave less a man made him more of a chattel" (p. 217).

Despite the amorphous character of the Negro's legal position, the Handlins noted that differential treatment was accorded the African. This, they state, was due to the settler's anxieties and insecurities which came in response to a strange environment. But it was also due in part, to "unique qualities in the African." In a descriptive paragraph, the Handlins partly undermine their original position:

The rudeness of the Negroes' manner, the strangeness of their languages, the difficulty of communicating to them English notions of morality and proper behavior occasioned sporadic laws to regulate their conduct (p. 208).

But these social antagonisms were not crucial to the Handlins' thesis. "Until the 1660's the statutes on the Negroes were not at all unique. Nor did they add up to a decided trend" (p. 209; n. 49).

When the Handlins turn to the development of slavery in the northern colonies, they note parallel developments of labor shortages, social distinctions, police regulations, and other factors which helped to define the Negro as chattel property.

In his analysis of the evolvement of slavery, Stanley Elkins concurs with the Handlins' view that there was nothing "natural" about its origins. *Slavery: A Problem in American Institutional and Intellectual Life* (Chicago: University of Chicago Press, 1959). For a concise synposis of the early historiographical debate, see pp. 38-41 (especially footnotes), which provide an institutional perspective to the problem. Although Elkins's thesis is similar to that asserted by the Handlins, he did not rule out the possibility of external influences. He rejects the Handlins' statement that Virginians could not have been affected by West Indian slavery, noting that in reponse to a large influx of Africans into Barbados the Governor's Council in 1636 declared that all Negroes and Indians were to serve as slaves for life.

Nevertheless, Elkins's interpretation rests on dynamic economic developments. The Negro's legal indeterminacy in the early decades of the seventeenth century is highly significant to Elkins for it suggests that the status of the Negro could conceivably have been otherwise. The few examples of free and propertied Negroes are sufficiently ample, he contends, "to convince one that even so small a margin between automatic lifetime slavery and something else made all the difference" (p. 41). On this point Elkins sides with Ames and Craven, who argued that in his "ill-defined" state there were no automatic guarantees for the Negro one way or the other. The Handlins, putting emphasis on the lack of differentiation between white servants and blacks, imply that the latter were on an equal footing with the former. Ames, Craven, and Elkins do not accept the proposition that the existence of free Negroes demonstrates the absence of status differentiation.

For Elkins, that "precious margin of space" which meant the difference between acceptance or rejection of the Negro as a free being crumbled rapidly in the middle of the century under the heavy blows of expanding capitalism. In colonial Virginia, he wrote, an agrarian capitalist organization was assuming "a purity of form never yet seen," in an environment "where no prior traditional institutions with competing claims of their own, might interfere at any of a dozen points with sufficient power to retard or modify its progress. What happens when such energy meets no limits?" (p. 43).

Elkins concluded that the rising capitalist class, confronted by increasing costs and declining profits in the decades of the 1660s and 1670s, turned to full use of the black in order to stabilize its labor supply. With the maturation of the large-scale, profit making plantation and in the absence of competing institutions such as the church or state, there was nothing "to prevent unmitigated capitalism from becoming unmitigated slavery. The planter was now engaged in capitalistic agriculture with a labor force entirely under his control" (p. 49). Thus, Elkins subscribed to the proposition that the denial of the black as a free person was essentially due to the unchallenged, expanding institution of capitalism and that the badge of an inferior status as laborer initiated and perpetuated prejudice.

Using an approach similar to the Handlins', cultural factors are subsidiary in Elkins's thesis. It is not that Elkins is unaware of social conflict—there is in fact a passage revealing acute sensitivity on his part to African-English relations—it is more that his approach is primarily an institutional one. Ignored, however, is the northern colonists' reaction to Africans. Elkins dismisses the statutory recognition of slavery in the North with a footnoted statement that as the number of Negroes was comparatively small, no effort was made requiring all blacks to comply with that condition.

In a striking challenge to Handlin and Elkins, Carl Degler reversed the causal relationships. In "Slavery and the Genesis of American Race Prejudice," *Comparative Studies in Society and History* Vol. 2 (October,

1959), p. 49-66 and *Out of Our Past* (New York: Harper & Row, 1959), Degler pointed to difficulties in the Handlins' position. Two flaws exist, stated Degler. First, the explanation of white servant improvement in Virginia in mid-century "cannot apply to New England, where servants were of minor importance . . . " The second major weakness in the Handlins' case "is the difficulty in showing that the white servant's position was improving during and immediately after the 1660s" (*Comparative Studies*, p. 51).

Degler returned to the basic position held by Ames and Craven but carried their argument to its logical conclusion, namely, that discrimination particularly preceded and affected the enslavement process. "If," exclaimed Degler, "instead of assuming that discrimination is a consequence of slavery, we work on the assumption that discrimination preceded slavery and thereby conditioned it . . . " then what happened fed on previous expressions, experiences, and images (*Out of Our Past*, p. 30). The origins of the racial problem lay in the discriminatory atmosphere of the early seventeenth century, an atmosphere which reflected a type of folk bias on the part of the settlers. There is a real possibility, Degler surmised, that "the Negro was actually never treated as an equal of the white man, servant or free" (*Comparative Studies* p. 51). Differences between the English and the Negro—in terms of biology, religion and culture—were the determinants which caused slavery. Given their attitudes toward and treatment of other groups, it was to be expected that the English would reject the African as an equal. In fact, the introduction of Africans as slaves into the colonies "unquestionably fostered a sense of superiority among Englishmen" (p. 31).

More important, Degler flatly disagreed with the Handlins and went beyond Elkins in declaring that the colonies on the seaboard had "ample opportunity to learn of discriminatory practices against Negroes from island settlements of Englishmen such as Bermuda and New Providence in the Caribbean." These practices, which restricted movement, trading and the bearing of arms, were legislated in the 1620s when the number of blacks was quite small.

What Degler alluded to, then, was a psychological response on the part of the English to other cultures. Degler was thus able to explain the passage of slave laws in the northern colonies in the early decades of the century. Like their southern counterparts, "New Englanders enacted into law, in the absence of any prior English law of slavery, their recognition of Negroes as different in race, religion and culture" (p. 38). So the equation was turned around. In Degler's view slavery must be absolved from starting the cycle. It was the discriminatory attitude and behavior which conditioned the form slavery would take (p. 38).

The Handlins responded to Degler in a sharply worked rebuttal. Citing confusions of terminology and misrepresentations on Degler's part, the Handlins restated their argument. Degler's longer reply is an excellent synthesis of his position. See their letters in *Comparative Studies in Society and History*, Vol. 2 (July, 1960), pp. 488-95.

In his study of the subject, "Modern Tensions and the Origins of American Slavery," *Journal of Southern History*, Vol. 28 (February, 1962). pp. 18-30, Winthrop Jordan tackled the question whether prejudice was the precursor of slavery or vice versa. Why, he asked, must it be an either/or proposition? What if both slavery and prejudice were reflections of a general debasement of the Negro? "Both may have been equally cause and effect, constantly reacting upon each other, dynamically joining hands to hustle the Negro down the road to degradation" (p. 29).

Interaction of these two processes began, Jordan noted, in the early part of the century. By the 1640s, slavery's most essential characteristics are to be found in actions which isolated the Negroes for special treatment: longer sentences in the courts for various violations of laws and customs, higher prices paid for blacks than for white servants, preference for black women as servants, and in other significant ways.

Jordan expanded his ideas in a prodigous work, *White Over Black: American Attitudes Toward the Negro, 1550-1812* (Chapel Hill: University of North Carolina Press, 1968) in which he traced English attitudes toward nonwhites prior to colonization. Jordan quickly noted that contact with Africans in the sixteenth century produced immediate reactions. "The most arresting characteristic of the newly discovered African was his color. Travelers rarely failed to comment upon it; indeed when describing Negroes they frequently began with complexion and then moved on to dress (or rather lack of it) and manners" (p. 4). Jordan observed that the English described the African in the specific term of *black*, which was "an exaggerated term which in itself suggests that the Negro's complexion had powerful impact upon their perceptions" (p. 5). Similarly, the African's religion, regarded as heathenism, "was at once a counter-image of their own religion and a summons to eradicate an important distinction between the two peoples" (p. 21). Thus, the thesis of early distinctions as propounded by Ames, Craven, and Degler was heavily and convincingly documented. "From the first," Jordan concluded, "Englishmen tended to set Negroes over against themselves, to stress what they conceived to be radically contrasting qualities of color, religion, and style of life, as well as animality and a peculiarly potent sexuality" (p. 43).

In his analysis of the establishment of slavery, Jordan was deeply concerned about the paucity of evidence, writing that the details of the process which produced the institution "can never be completely reconstructed; there is simply not enough evidence (and very little chance of more to come) to show precisely when and how and why Negroes came to be treated so differently from white men, though there is just enough to make historians differ as to its meaning" (p. 44). Especially did Jordan express misgivings about the lack of knowledge of early reactions towards blacks in the first decade. Nonetheless, Jordan was somewhat sympathetic to the labor view of enslavement, holding that "Negroes became slaves, partly because there were social and economic necessities in America which called for some sort of bound, controlled labor" (p. 61). But the nub of his thesis, in a chapter entitled "Unthinking Decision," was contained in his article. "Taken as a whole, the evidence reveals a process of debasement of which hereditary lifetime service was an important but not the only part" (p. 80). Jordan contrasts enslavement in Virginia and Maryland with the process which occurred in other British colonies. The available data, he notes, "points to less borrowing and to this kind of process: a mutually interactive growth of slavery and unfavorable assessment, with no cause for either which did not cause the other as well" (p. 80).

Jordan's insight into English attitudes and the concept of blackness was complemented by a work which concentrated more fully on the use of the African in English drama. Eldred Jones's *Othello's Countrymen* (Oxford: Oxford University Press, 1965) examined the African image in sixteenth-century England, with particular emphasis on the dramatic treatments of African characters, use of language, and the physical portrayals in plays. Jones demonstrates the extensive usage of the African by Elizabethan and Jacobean playwrights, the ultimate expression being the hero in Shakespeare's *Othello*.

The problem of just how the first Africans were received went largely unexplored until Alden T. Vaughan focused on the subject. Vaughan was not as disheartened by the scarcity of information as others. In his article, "Blacks in Virginia: A Note on the First Decade", *William and Mary*

*Quarterly*, 3rd ser. Vol. 34 (July, 1972), pp. 469-78, Vaughan pointedly suggested that information for the 1620s regarding the first blacks was "not so lacking or unrevealing as has been supposed" (p. 469). For Vaughan, the data supported, "with disturbing clarity," the contention that from the beginning blacks held "a singularly debased status in the eyes of white Virginians. If not subjected to permanent and inheritable bondage during the decade—a matter that needs further evidence—black Virginians were at least well on their way to such a condition" (pp. 469-70). Analyzing the data from two colony-wide censuses taken in the 1620s, Vaughan observed that blacks received the scantiest and most impersonal entries compared to other groups. Moreover, in the 1625 census, none of the blacks were listed as being free; all were counted as "servants" (p. 476).

Warren M. Billings, in delving into "The Cases of Fernando and Elizabeth Key: A Note on the Status of Blacks in Seventeenth-Century Virginia," *William and Mary Quarterly*, 3rd ser. Vol. 30 (July, 1973), pp. 467-74, further buttressed the proposition of early differentiation but also demonstrated how religion affected black status. The two cases show that although prejudice and antagonisms were constant determinants, the colonists had allowed some blacks to escape bondage through legal means. "Their religion and their paternity were of crucial importance for determining which blacks should become servants" (p. 473). But once whites had perceived blacks— Billings emphasized "free blacks" in this instance though it is not entirely clear why—and miscengenation as undermining the colony, they acted to limit the African's "approaches to liberty" (p. 474).

In the early seventies, George Frederickson brought a different conception to the problem. In "Towards a Social Interpretation of the development of American Racism," *Key Issues in the Afro-American Experience*, eds. Nathan I. Huggins, Martin Kilson and Daniel M. Fox, (New York: Harcourt, Brace, Jovanovich, 1971), pp. 240-54, he isolated two different aspects of racism and found the Ames-Degler-Jordan thesis insufficient, if not erroneous in explaining the origins and development of slavery and racism in the United States. It should be noted, through, that Frederickson thought Jordan's interactive view that slavery and race prejudice continuously reacted upon each other, was "clearly the last work" (p. 244). Frederickson distinguished between "the explicit and rationalized racism that can be discerned in nineteenth- and early twentieth-century thought and ideology and the implicit or societal racism that can be *inferred* from actual social relationships" (pp. 240-41). Importantly, one type of racism can function without the other; that is, "implicit racism can exist without explicit racism; indeed, events in the twentieth century suggest that societal racism can continue to thrive long after ideological racism has been discredited . . . " (p. 241). What historians have done, explained Frederickson, is to assume that the explicit or ideological racism—"the formal doctrine of inherent biological inferiority"— which was in vogue later in American history flourished very early in the seventeenth century. The question for Frederickson was: "to what extent was America really born racist as a result of pre-existing attitudes and to what extent did it become so as a result of social, economic, and political developments which took place well after the colonists' initial contacts with Africans?" (p. 242). The answer he gave counters the generally accepted thesis that America was "born racist." Rather, "it became so gradually as the result of a series of crimes against black humanity that stemmed primarily from selfishness, greed, and the pursuit of privilege" (p. 254).

Frederickson's parting with the early racism thesis begins with his interpretation of the seventeenth-century English. Though he agrees that the prevailing stereotype of the African was "unfavorable," this connoted prejudice rather than societal racism. Moreover, Frederickson surmised that the stereotypes about Africans "held by some Englishmen on the eve of colonization were opinions casually held," opinions that would not necessarily lead to societal racism (p. 243). That would take a catalyst in the form of a fear, the nature of which could be described in social terms. Specifically, these social factors were black vulnerability, white aristocratic efforts toward defining a social order, and status jockeying. These provided the ingredients for a full-fledged societal racism which later came to represent racial attitudes.

Donald Noel, a sociologist interested in ethnic stratification, has developed a theoretical construct to explain the origins of slavery. Noel's purpose in "A Theory of the Origin of Ethnic Stratification," *Social Problems*, Vol. 16 (Fall, 1968), pp. 157-72; reprinted in *The Origins of American Slavery and Racism*, ed. Donald L. Noel (Columbus, Oh.: Charles E. Merrill Publishing Co., 1972), pp. 106-27, is to present a theory of the origin of ethnic stratification which also illuminates "the known facts regarding the origin of American slavery" (p. 106). Three crucial variables comprise Noel's thesis: ethnocentrism, competition, and differential power. The absence of any of these factors, Noel noted, means that ethnic stratification will not emerge.

In the instance of the enslavement of the black in the seventeenth century, Noel observed, all three variables were in operation. Noel maintained first, that blacks were the object of "a relatively intense rejection from the beginning." Secondly, mobility created "an arena of competition" which complemented ethnocentric emotions. The focal point of the competition was labor, coveted because it provided prestige and wealth. Concomitantly, blacks suffered from their vulnerability. Significantly, and unfortunately, Noel pointed out, "the rigidity of the 'peculiar institution' was fixed before the Negroes acquired sufficient common culture, sense of shared fate, and identity to be able to effectively challenge the system" (pp. 121-22).

For a concise survey of the debate, see the essay in the first-rate bibliography by James M. McPherson, Laurence B. Holland, James M. Banner, Jr., Nancy J. Weiss and Michael D. Bell, *Blacks in America: Bibliographical Essays* (New York: Doubleday & Co., 1971), pp. 39-42. Noel's article, "A Theory of the Origin . . . " also contains a broad interpretation of the issues.

## The Indian & The Servant

Two comparative histories provide insight into early ethnic relationships and conflicts. Wesley Frank Crave, *White, Red, and Black: The Seventeenth Century Virginian* (University Press of Virginia, 1971), a compilation of three essays, neatly etched the differences between the three cultures and offered important land patent head rights data for determining the black population in Virginia. More complex and encompassing is Gary Nash's superb work about ethnic history in the northeastern colonies, *Red, White and Black: The Peoples of Early America* (New York: Prentice-Hall, 1974). Nash's work is an essential starting point for a study of cultural conflict and racism in North America. His discerning analysis of attitudes towards the Indian in the South can be found in "The Image of the Indian in the Southern Colonial Mind," *William and Mary Quarterly*, 3rd ser., Vol. 29 (April 1972), pp. 197-230. Additionally, Winthrop Jordan's *The White Man's Burden: Historical Origins of Racism in the United States* (Oxford: Oxford University Press, 1974) must be consulted. Though it is, in Jordan's words, a "drastic abridgement with minor modifications," of his work, *White Over Black*, it contains relevant material concerning attitudes toward the Indian. See also Almon W. Lauber, *Indian Slavery in Colonial Times Within the Present Limits of the United States* (New York: Columbia Univeristy Press, 1913).

English preoccupations regarding the savage nature and habits of the Indian are stated in *Hakluytus Postumus, or Purchas His Pilgrimes* (Glasgow, 1906), Vol. 19, pp. 218-65. The excellent work by Roy Harvey Pearce, *The Savages of America: A Study of the Indian and the Idea of Civilization* (Baltimore: Johns Hopkins Press, 1953), especially chapter 1, provides an analysis of English conceptions of civilization as they relate to missionary motivations and relations with the Indians. Nancy Oestreich Lurie, "Indian Cultural Adjustment to European Civilization," and Wilcomb E. Washburn, "The Moral and Legal Justification for Dispossessing the Indian," in *Seventeenth Century America*, ed. James Morton Smith, analyze English-Indian conflict and detail the arguments for English subjugation.

The significance of education to civility can be found in the essay by James Brinsley, the noted sixteenth-century schoolmaster, in his "Consolations for Our Grammar Schools" in *The Transit of Civilization*, by Edward Eggleston (New York: D. Appleton Co.: 1901). Bernard Bailyn's provocative volume, *Education in the Forming of American Society* (Chapel Hill: University of North Carolina Press, focuses on attitudes towards children and education as the means by which they can be "saved." Education was a crucial cultural nexus. The best overall view of education in the early period . is in Lawrence A Cremin, *American Education: The Colonial Experience* (New York: Columbia University Press, 1973).

The colonial attempt to educate the Indian is well detailed by W. Stitt Robonson, Jr., "Indian Education and Missions in Colonial Virginia," *The Journal of Sourthern History* Vol. 27 (May, 1952), pp. 152-68. A very good scholarly work on the subject is Sadie Bell, *The Church, The State and Education in Virginia* (1930; reprint ed., New York: Arno Press, 1969). See also the article by Robert H. Land, "Henrico and Its College," *William and Mary Quarterly*, 2nd ser., Vol 28 (1938), pp. 453-98. Additional information relating to colonial efforts can be found in Elsie W. Clews, *Educational Legislation and Administration of the Colonial Governments* (New York: Macmillan Co., 1899); S. M. Kingsbury, ed., *Records of the Virginia Company*, 4 vols. (Washington, D.C.: Library of Congress, 1906); and Philip A. Bruce, *Institutional History of Virginia in the Seventeenth Century*, 2 vols. (New York: G. P. Putnam's Sons, 1910).

Most approaches to this subject concentrate on English efforts to instruct the Indian. James Axtell, in "The Scholastic Philosophy of the Wilderness", *William and Mary Quarterly*, 3rd ser., Vol. 29 (July, 1972), pp. 335-66, correctly noted that education is a mutual process and focused upon lessons the English learned from the Indian. Axtell wrote that the Indian performed multivaried roles, as neighbor, warrior, and teacher, and provided lessons for the English, which "ironically, helped tip that scale against the Indians' own future" (p. 336).

Compilations of legislation and laws relating to education in the colonial period are few in number. Among the best are Paul Monroe, *Founding of the American Public School System II*, (Ann Arbor: University Microfilms, 1940) and Clews,

An early standard and informative work on the white indentured labor system is James C. Ballagh, *White Servitude in the Colony of Virginia* (Burt Franklin, 1895). Marcus W. Jernegan, *Laboring and Dependent Classes in Colonial America 1607-1783* (New York: Columbia University Press, 1946) and Abbot E. Smith, *Colonists in Bondage: White Servitude and Convict Labor in America, 1607-1776* (Chapel Hill: University of North Carolina Press, 1947) are indispensable works. Richard Hofstadter, in *America at 1750: A Social Portrait* (New York: Alfred A. Knopf, 1971) also provides a graphic but capsulated overview of bondage; see chapter 2.

One of the rewarding views of the social life of the Virginia colony in the first decades as it relates to labor conditions and issues is Edmund S. Morgan's "The First American Boom: Virginia 1618-1630," *William and Mary Quarterly* 3rd ser., Vol. 28 (April 1971), pp. 169-98.

## The Education

With very few exceptions the studies on slavery barely mention seventeenth-century black education other than to point out that some slaves were accorded some training and instruction. One exception is Jernegan's *Laboring and Dependent Classes in America*, which reprinted a document written in 1649, "A Perfect Description of Virginia" in which the author gives a detailed account of the procedures by which slaves were to be taught artisan skills and the performance of simple manufacturing tasks. Susie M. Ames, in a tightly written essay, *Reading, Writing and Arithmetic in Virginia, 1607-1699* (Williamsburg, Va., 1957; Historical Booklet, Number 15) touches lightly on the subject. Bell, in *The Church, the State and Education in Virginia*, also mentions black education.

The fullest account on the subject is provided by Cremin in his excellent work *American Education: The Colonial Experience*. Guy Fred Wells, *Parish Education in Colonial Virginia* (New York: Columbia University Press, 1923) is an ample treatment of education in Virginia parishes but does not consider the African. Virtually all other studies begin their accounts in the eighteenth century.

## The Name

Afro-American genealogy is a vast and fruitful field which has long been neglected. *Names*, the journal devoted to the subject, has had only one significant article published in the area since its inception.

The folklorist, Newbell Niles Puckett, began a systematic study of black names many years ago and published a significant article, "Names of American Negro Slaves," in *Studies in the Science of Society*, ed. George P. Murdock, (New Haven, Conn.: Yale University Press, 1937), pp. 471-94. His data and findings have been somewhat expanded and updated in a work by an historian, Murray Heller, ed., *Black Names in America: Origins and Usage Collected by Newbell Niles Puckett* (G. K. Hall, 1974).

An article which offers the most suggestive data is J. L. Dillard, "The West African Day-Names in Nova-Scotia," *Names*, Vol. 19 (September, 1971), pp. 257-61. Dillard contends that the language and culture of Afro-Americans of Nova Scotia from 1750 "turns out to be very much like those found in the United States" (p. 258). There is considerable evidence in Dillard's piece which indicates that Africans were able to use their day-names with some success despite their vulnerability. Unfortunately, his research begins with the mid-eighteenth century. His impressive work is *Black English: Its History and Usage in the United States* (New York: Random House, 1972).

Other studies which deal with the general subject are Arthur P. Hudson, "Some Curious Negro Names," *Southern Folklore Quarterly*, Vol. 2 (December, 1938), pp. 179-93; Howard F. Barker, "The Family Names of American Negroes," *American Speech*, Vol. 14 (October, 1939), pp. 163-74; Hennig Cohen, "Slave Names in Colonial South Carolina," *American Speech*, Vol. 28 (1952), pp. 102-107.

Since his successful search of personal lineage, Alex Haley has organized the Kinte Foundation. The foundation is researching in three main areas:

recording the "great tradition" of West Africa; securing archival data on shipping manifests; and conducting an oral history in the Northeast, Sea Islands, New Orleans and in the region of Virginia-Washington-Maryland. For a fuller explanation of Haley's historical exploration and the foundation's objectives, see Alex Haley, "Black History, Oral History and Genealogy," and Courtney Brown, "Oral History and the Oral Tradition, Black America, The Kinte Foundation," in *The Oral History Review*, (New York: Oral History Association, 1973—, pp. 1-25; 26-28.

## The Decisions, The Law

Many of the studies on the origins of slavery in Virginia deal in some fashion with pertinent legal cases and decisions. An indispensable source is William W. Henings's *Statutues at Large: A Collection of all the Laws of Virginia*, (13 Vols. 1823; reprinted., Unversity Press of Virginia, 1969), the first three volumes of which cover the period from 1619 to 1710. Hening's volumes are a chronological listing of all of the laws of the colony. By contrast, Helen T. Catterall's *Judicial Cases Concerning American Slavery and the Negro*, 5 vols. (1926; reprinted., New York: Octagon Books, 1968), Vol. 1, 53-81, contains both an historical text and an abridged listing of cases relating to the Negro. An important in-depth examination of the gradual process of enslavement is in Paul C. Palmer, "Servant into Slave: The Evolution of the Legal Status of the Negro Laborer in Colonial Virginia," *South Atlantic Quarterly*, Vol. 65 (Summer, 1966), pp. 355-70. Palmer concluded that the early laws would not lead one to believe that members of the assembly were actually prescribing slavery; rather, the laws "seem more often to be describing and giving quasi-legal sanction to practices already in existence" (p. 370). The work by Jonathan L. Alpert adds an important dimension on the Maryland situation: "The Origin of Slavery in the United States: The Maryland Precedent," *American Journal of Legal History*, Vol. 14 (July, 1970). pp. 189-221. A dissertation on "The Criminal Law of Slavery and Freedom, 1860-1868," by Daniel Flanigan (Rice University; May, 1973), handles the issues in significant perspective.

# Index

Africa, Africans, 26-27
   day-names, 33, 35
   theatre stereotypes, 27
   West African slaves, 27, 33-34
Africanus, John Leo, 27
Andros, Gov. Edmund, 13
Apprenticeship statutes, 23
Arbuthnot, John, 62
Arnold, James, 30
Assimilation, acculturation, 4, 5, 18, 52
Axtell, George, 33

Bailyn, Bernard, 20
Bell, Daniel, 5
Bell, Sadie, 87
Berkeley, Gov. William, 26, 46
Berry, Brewton, 7
Black Muslims, 34
Blackness, European attitudes toward, 26-28
Blair, Rev. James, 24
Brinkley, John, 21
Burdett, William, 42
Butler, Samuel, 28

Calvert, Leonard, 30, 88
Caribbean, slavery in, 4, 69
Catterall, Helen T., 38
Censuses, of slaves and servants, 26-27
Children:
   English names for, 30-31
   Indian, 9, 12-13, 76

Children (continued)
   inherited status of, 43-45
   interracial, 46-47, 97
   and willed property, 19, 78-79
   *See also* Education; Religious instruction
Community life, tension in, 18-19
Conflict, cultural, 7
Connecticut:
   education laws, 21
   Indian schools, 13, 74
   slave laws, 46
Courts, 19. *See also* Laws, legislation
Crashaw, William, 8, 58-60
Craven, Wesley Frank, 26
Cremin, Lawrence, 6-7, 13-14, 19, 24
Cuffee, Paul, 33
Culpeper, Lord Thomas, 13

Davies, Sir John, 61
Davis, Hugh, 39
Denham, Sir John, 61
Drama, black stereotypes in, 27
Dryden, John, 28, 57, 61
Duke's Law (N.Y., 1664), 21, 81

Education, 18-25, 52-53, 85-86. *See also*
   Religious instruction
   and colonization, 19
   of Indians, 9-10, 12-14, 66-68, 76-77
   of slaves, 23-25
Education laws, 20-24, 80, 81
Elizabeth I, Queen, 27

England:
    African population in, 27
    blackness, attitudes towards, 26-28
    ethnocentrism, 7, 18, 35, 63-65, 72
    racial perceptions, 7-8, 10-11, 26-28,
        63-65, 72
    slavery in, 4
    social distance in, 51-53
English slave names, 30-31, 35
Equiano, Olaudah, 35, 89
Ethnocentrism, of English colonists,
    7-11, 18, 35, 63-65, 72

Fleetwood, Bishop William, 24
Fox, George, 24
Franklin, Benjamin, 14, 75-77
Free blacks, 41, 46-47, 49, 51, 92
    laws for, 47, 49, 94-95
    as slave holders, 47, 48, 92

Godwyn, Morton, 3, 4, 20
Golding, William, 22-23
Goodhand, Capt. Marmaduke, 30

Hakluyt, Richard, 9, 27
Haley, Alex, 33-34
Hamor, Ralph, 33
Handlin, Mary, 4
Handlin, Oscar, 4, 18
Harmer, Charles, 43
Harvard College, 13-14
Henrico College (Va.), 10, 11, 66, 67-68
Herbert, George, 29

Indentured servants, 14-16, 39
    censuses, 26
    and free black masters, 47, 92
    prices, 42-43
    and the tobacco economy, 14-15
Indian place names, 33
Indians, 3-5, 6-14, 51
    children, 9, 12-13, 76
    education of, 9-10, 12-14, 66-68,
        76-77
    English counterattacks, 11, 72-73
    English perceptions of, 7-8, 10-11, 63,
        64-65, 72
    kidnapping of, 12
    massacres by, 69, 72
    ordinances for, 11, 45-46, 70
    religious instruction of, 8, 9, 12
    "savagery" of, 18, 22, 63, 69
    and slavery, 12, 13, 43, 46, 94-95
Intermarriage. See Miscegenation

James I, King, 10, 21
Johnson, Dr. Samuel, 28, 57, 61-62
Jordon, Winthrop, 28

Keith, George, 24
Key, Elizabeth, 42

Laws, legislation, 3-4, 38-39. See also
        Punishment
    apprenticeship statutes, 23
    education, 20-23, 80
    Indian, 11, 45-46, 70
    killing of slaves, 45, 91, 96
    manumission, 46-47, 49, 97
    miscegenation, 46-47, 96-97
    racial distinctions, 43-46, 47, 92,
        94-95
    religious factors, 40-42, 45
    religious instruction, 80, 81
    for runaways, 15, 39-40, 90, 96-97
    sexual restrictions, 39, 44
    weapons, prohibition of, 39, 47, 49, 93
Literature, blacks and blackness in, 27-28
Locke, John, 62
London Company, 9
Lurie, Nancy Oestreich, 10

Malcolm X, 34-35
Mann, Horace, 18
Manning, Edward, 29
Manumission laws, 46-47, 49, 97
Maryland, slave laws of, 3-4, 46, 47
Massachusetts, laws of, 20-21, 46
Mather, Cotton, 32
Milton, John, 57
Miscegenation, 3, 39
    laws, 46-47, 96-97
Morgan, Edmund, 16
Mynor, John, 74
Mynor, Thomas, 74

Names, naming, 29-36
    African, 32-35, 89
    English, 30-31, 35
    identity, denial of, 32-35
    Indian, 33
    Spanish, 30-32, 35
    surnames, 31-33, 35, 43
Nash, Gary B., 8, 10
New Amsterdam. See New York
New England:
    Indian schools in, 13-14
    preservation of culture, 19
New Jersey, slave laws in, 46

New York:
    education laws, 21, 81
    Indian schools, 13
    religious instruction, 22, 81
    slave laws, 46
Nicholson, Gov. Francis, 53

Orphans, education of, 19-20, 78-79

Philips, John, 62
Pierce, Capt. William, 39
Pocahontas, 33
Pope, Alexander, 57
Portugal, racism in, 7
Pory, John, 15
Pott, Francis, 43
Punishment, 15
    runaways, 39-40, 92, 93, 96
    whippings, 47, 92

Racism:
    blackness, symbolism of, 26-28
    and education of slaves, 23-25
    in Elizabethan England, 27
    in laws, 43-46, 47, 92, 94-95
Raleigh, Sir Walter, 57
Religious instruction, 21, 40-41
    baptism, 41
    of Indians, 8, 9, 12
    laws, 80
    of slaves, 24, 87
    social benefits, 41-42
Robinson, John, 22, 82-86
Rolfe, John, 7, 33
Runaways, laws for, 15, 39-40, 44-45, 90,
    96-97

Segregation policies, 5
Sermons, 8, 58-60
Servants. See Indentured servants
Sewall, Samuel, 32
Sexual restrictions, 39, 44
Shakespeare, 28, 57
Skin color, symbolism of, 27-28
Skinner, John, 30, 88
Slaves:
    censuses, 26-27
    as chattel property, 4, 53
    Christian slaves, 40-41
    legal status of, 38
    naming of, 29-36
    ownership, 46, 94-95
    prices, 42-43, 44
    religious instruction, 24, 87

Slaves (continued)
    runaways, 15, 39-40, 44-45, 90, 96-97
    See also Free blacks
Slavery:
    contracts, 88
    education and, 23-25
    and English culture, 51-52
    and the Indians, 12, 13, 94-95
    legalization of, 47-49, 94-95
    length of service, 43-44
    and manumission, 41, 46-47, 49, 97
    revolts, mutinies, 15
Smith, John, 9, 11, 33, 63, 69
Society for the Propagation of the Gospel
    in Foreign Parts, 14, 24
South Carolina, slave laws in, 46
Spanish colonies, slavery and racism in, 4,
    7, 69
Spanish names, 30-32, 35
Spenser, Edmund, 61
Spratt, Thomas, 57
Stone, James, 42
Suleiman, Ayuba, 34, 35
Sweet, Robert, 39, 44
Swift, Jonathan, 61

Tobacco economy, and indentured servants,
    14-15
Tocqueville, Alexis de, 3, 6

Unfreedom, concept of, 4

Vaughn, Richard, 24
Virginia:
    black censuses, 26-27
    education laws, 20, 21, 23-24, 80
    Indian attacks (1622), 10, 11, 69-73
    Indian ordinances, 11, 70
    slave legislation, 3-4
    See also Laws, legislation
Virginia Charter, Letters Patent of (1606), 8
Virginia Company, 9, 15

Walker, Maj. Peter, 42-43
Waller, Edmund, 61
Waltham, John, 20
Weapons, laws prohibiting, 39, 47, 49, 93
West Africa, slaves from, 27, 33-34
White servants. See Indentured servants
Whitehead, Thomas, 46
Whittington, William, 43
William and Mary College, 13, 24

Yeardley, George, 66